BLOG
FOR
BUCKS

How to Create, Promote, and Profit from Your Blog

JACQUELINE BODNAR

ALLWORTH PRESS
NEW YORK

Allworth Press books may be purchased in bulk at special discounts for sales promotion, corporate gifts, fund-raising, or educational purposes. Special editions can also be created to specifications. For details, contact the Special Sales Department, Allworth Press, 307 West 36th Street, 11th Floor, New York, NY 10018 or info@skyhorsepublishing.com.

24 23 22 21 20   5 4 3 2 1

Published by Allworth Press, an imprint of Skyhorse Publishing, Inc. 307 West 36th Street, 11th Floor, New York, NY 10018. Allworth Press® is a registered trademark of Skyhorse Publishing, Inc.®, a Delaware corporation.

www.allworth.com

Cover design by Mary Ann Smith

Library of Congress Cataloging-in-Publication Data is available on file.

Print ISBN: 978-1-62153-770-0
eBook ISBN: 978-1-62153-771-7

Printed in the United States of America

"Books are the most powerful tool in the human arsenal."
—Will Schwalbe

For Brian, Kayla, and Tristan . . . my loves.

Contents

Blogging Basics

In choosing to read this book, you have made the decision to learn about something new, which is great. Many people are interested in blogging, but are intimidated, assuming that it's something difficult to learn. They fear that they will have to know how to program or code, or that they won't be able to come up with blog post ideas. Yet amidst their fear, they are still intrigued. They have heard about blogs, know bloggers who make a living from their blogging, and want to know if they could do it, too.

In short, yes, you can do it, too. Making money from blogging is not all that difficult. Yes, there is a short learning curve to blogging, but that goes for anything new in life that you want to learn. Whether you are taking Zumba or yoga, playing a sport, or learning a new language, there is always a learning curve. If you don't let the fear of that learning curve hold you back, then you will not only be able to learn how to blog, but you can thrive at doing so. There are millions of bloggers making money from their blogging. Some do it as a full-time job, while others do it as a side hustle. Either way, the earnings potential is there for everyone who wants to apply themselves and learn how to make it happen.

I started blogging in 2009 and since that time have grown several popular blogs, and earn money from them every month. Throughout the pages of this book, I will share with you what I've learned from my own blogging experiences, as well as information that I've gathered from other sources and bloggers. Combined, all of this information should help calm any anxiety you may have about blogging, and provide you with the confidence you need to succeed at it.

BLOGS DEFINED

Some people who picked up this book may be familiar with what blogs are. They may even have a blog and are looking for ways to make their blog more lucrative or successful. However, there are some people who are reading this who are familiar with the term, but are newer to the concept of a blog, which makes it necessary to start with the blogging basics.

A blog is a web log; it's a website where most of the pages that are added are posts, and they are all dated in reverse chronological order. With the posts being dated in reverse chronological order, the older posts are pushed further down, with the newer posts being on top. Picture a blog like a spiral notebook journal. Every time you add a page, or post, to your journal, you are adding a new sheet of paper to the top of the stack. The newer posts get layered on top of the older ones, and the whole journal stays in a dated order, with the newer posts on top. A blog works in much the same way, only it's online, so you can't see the posts all stacked up on top of each other like you would in a notebook.

Blogs are used for a wide variety of things beyond just sharing your own personal musings. There are people who have random blogs, where they may share their thoughts about a wide variety of issues, but there are many more blogs that have a more defined focus. There is no limit to the variety and subjects that are covered on blogs. People blog about everything and anything, and there is usually an audience for whatever your subject of choice may be.

Millions of people are independent bloggers, who choose a topic that they are passionate about and focus their efforts on that one subject. They may blog about French cuisine, entertainers, technology, flowers, hiking, or any number of other things. These blogs tend to offer many posts that relate to that one topic. There are also blogs that cover a wider variety of topics, and those that are extensions of a business. Many businesses have blogs so that they can help drive traffic to their website, keep in touch with their potential customers, and establish themselves as an authority. Blogs can be a great way for businesses to bring in more customers.

It's believed that the first blog was created in 1994. It was just a few years later that the term "weblog" was coined, giving this type of website a name. Then a couple of years after that, the "we" was dropped, giving the websites the official name that we know them by today, a blog. Now, twenty-five years after that first blog was created, there are millions of blogs online. They have become an easy way for people to share their thoughts, create an income, grow their businesses, and keep in touch.

No matter what topic you want to focus on, it's important that you continue to keep blogging. Just as there are millions of blogs today, there are also millions of blogs that have been started and then sit, going nowhere. *Blogging* is a verb; it's something you have to do, and keep up on doing. If you start a blog, create a few posts, and then walk away, your blog isn't going to become much of anything. In order to have a successful blog, you have to continuously be active with it. By that, I mean you will need to create regular posts, so that new content is published with some degree of regularity. If you don't, your blog will be stagnant and most likely die.

Going into blogging, be aware that if you want it to be successful and to bring in an income, you have to continue to keep it active. That doesn't mean you need to create five posts per day, but it does mean that you shouldn't go months without it getting any new posts, either. There is no magic number of posts you should do per week or month in order to have a successful blog that receives a decent amount of traffic. You will need to find the right balance for you regarding posting with regularity.

One of the beautiful things about a blog is that it has the voice of the blogger, or of multiple bloggers. There are some blogs that will have posts that remain neutral and just focus on getting the information out there, kind of how a news article should be. But most blogs tend to have the voice of the blogger who is behind the posts. That's how readers get to know the blogger and become fans. With a blog, you have more leeway in being able to infuse your personality into your posts. Some blogs have multiple bloggers who contribute to it, so the blog offers a variety of voices.

PICKING YOUR FOCUS

You may already have a focus in mind for your blog. If you are a health trainer, you may have a plan to create a health-focused blog. Foodies may opt for creating food blogs where they review restaurant meals; photography buffs may opt for a blog where they share about their work; travel enthusiasts may want to share about their trips; and so on. Most people probably already have some ideas of things they would like to blog about. Even if you think it's a topic that won't have much of an audience, you should give it a try. You may just be surprised at how many other people out there love what it is that you love, and by blogging you will essentially find your people. Or rather, they will find you.

Some people worry about starting a blog focusing on a topic that is already filled with too many bloggers. Don't let the competition keep you from starting your blog. It doesn't matter how many other people are blogging about a particular topic that is of interest to you. If you are interested in the topic, it doesn't make a difference if there are a million others covering the same topic. Your blog will be unique in that it is yours and it's going to have your voice, views, and focus. Perhaps you also know things about blogging that others don't, which will give you an edge in getting noticed and building a following. The only way that your blog will absolutely not be successful due to the competition is if it makes you not start it at all. Lose the fear and focus on the overall goals.

My grandfather owned a business for thirty-five years. He taught me many lessons in life, and one of the last ones he taught me before he died was to never worry about the competition. It's something that I took to heart and live by. I never worry about who my competition is or what they may be doing. Following his advice, I only focus on what I'm doing. Every minute you spend focusing on the competition is one less minute you are focusing on your own success. There are people who spend a lot of time watching their competition, trying to follow what they do, trying to do things to beat them, and more. To me, it's simply wasted energy to keep focusing on the competition. Plus, it doesn't feel good. Notice how you feel when you next spend time seeing what your competition is up to.

I believe my grandfather was right. Forget worrying about the competition, and just focus on your goals and mission. Your time and energy will be better spent. If you are looking for ideas for things you want to do on your blog, then by all means, check out some other blogs. But don't get hung up on competition, and once you have your blog established, avoid looking at competitor blogs. You do you, and do it with positive energy and determination. The rest will fall into place.

So, your first step is to determine what your blog is going to be about. If you have the idea in your mind, great, then you are set and ready to get started. If you just know you want to blog, but have no idea what to blog about, now is the time to start evaluating some of your interests. Make a list of five things that you love to talk about and love to do. You could conceivably start blogs on every one of those topics, and many bloggers do have more than one blog. But choose one of them to get started with. Which one do you think you will most enjoy writing about and exploring? Keep in mind that you will want a topic that you will be writing about a lot. I have blogs that have more than one thousand posts, and I have some that have more than six thousand posts.

SETTING UP YOUR BLOG

Once you know what the focus of your blog will be, it's time to choose a name and web address for it. Your blog needs an online address, also called a uniform resource locator (URL). Many sites that host blogs will allow you to simply create a name that is an extension of their website name. For example, you could create a travel blog with the address of something like *www.mytravelposts.bloghost.com*. However, it's better to have your own unique URL. Not only is it easier, but it's less cluttered and looks more professional.

Your blog will need to be hosted online, which means that a company is providing the storage of the files, and may be providing the blogging tool that you use to create and maintain your blog. Depending on what blog host company you choose to go with, you can register your own unique domain name with them, or you can go online and do it with another company, such as Network Solutions or GoDaddy. You will pay a small fee to register the URL in your name. You can choose to pay for multiple years at once, or you will need to make sure you renew the URL before the one-year mark is up.

When you register your blog name, you will most likely have to play around with different combinations to come up with something you like. This is because there are so many domain names that have been taken already. Don't get discouraged, though. Just keep at it until you find one that you really like. You are probably familiar with website addresses that end with .com, since that is the most popularly used. There are other extensions you can consider, such as .us, .info, .biz, and .fun, among others. When it comes to choosing a URL, simple is better. Try to get one that is simple and easy for people to remember.

Once you have paid for the domain name, or URL, that you want to use, you are ready to go on to setting up your blog.

BLOGGING PLATFORMS

To have a blog, you are going to have to pay someone to host the site. You will need to choose a blogging platform, which is where your site will be stored and managed. There are numerous ones to choose from, with some being more popular than others, and the prices for using each ranging quite a bit. It's a good idea to explore the various types of blogging platforms before signing up with one, so you can compare what each one offers, what the price is to use it, and so on.

Here are some of the more popular blogging platforms you may want to consider using:

- **WordPress.** This is the most popular option used by bloggers. In fact, its website states that it provides the platform for over 34 percent of all sites online. When you consider how many sites are online, you can get an idea of just how popular this platform is. WordPress is the software that you would use for blogging, but you also need a website host, which is where everything from your site will be stored. Those who use WordPress tend to use a lot of plug-ins, which are software components that allow you to do a lot of customization on your site. In fact, WordPress offers over fifty-five thousand plug-ins. While you can use WordPress for free, some of the plug-ins cost money to use. One of the downsides of using WordPress and all the plug-ins is that when there are plug-in updates, things can go wrong and it crashes your site. If you are tech-savvy, you may be able to fix it yourself. If not, you may end up spending money to get tech help to get your site back online. WordPress offers nice-looking templates to use, as well as providing you with ways to customize your site. If you go with a WordPress blog, you will need to find a place to have the content hosted. You will pay monthly or yearly hosting fees.
- **Typepad.** This is a blogging platform marketed to the non-technical person who wants to blog. Within minutes after signing up, you can pick a template and be writing your first post. It really has a simple system to use that most people should feel comfortable using without having a technical background. For around fifteen dollars per month, you can create as many blogs as you want with Typepad, and that includes using its software tool and hosting services.
- **Blogger.** Owned by Google, it offers a basic blogging tool that doesn't offer much in the way of customization. The number of templates is also limited. The draw for new bloggers to consider using this platform is that it's free to use. You can start as many blogs as you want, and it's an all-in-one service, giving you the blogging tool and hosting your

site. The platform is limited in what it offers, but is also simple to use, and again, being free may be enticing.

- **Wix.** It offers blog templates and hosting, starting at around seventeen dollars per month. It does limit how much storage space you get for your blog, and the rate is also for just one blog.
- **Squarespace.** They offer blogging software and hosting services, with pricing starting at around twelve dollars per month for one blog.

There are many other blogging platforms that you can also consider. What you want to look for in choosing which one is right for you is that the cost fits your budget, that you can have your own unique domain name and template designs, and whether storage is limited. It's important to have unlimited storage because as your blog continues to grow, you don't want to have to worry about surpassing some space allotments, or having to pay more.

A template is a blog design that is readily available for you to choose and use. Templates make it simple for nontechnical people to have a blog because you don't have to create the site from scratch. Someone else has created the template, and you will just fill in the information and do some customization. Most blogging platforms offer a range of templates you can choose from, so you can find something that fits your style and taste. Even with templates, you can usually make some changes in order to give it a more custom feel. With most templates, you can change the pictures, font, colors, and more. Depending on the blogging platform you choose, you may be able to purchase additional templates to use, have one custom-created for you, or use your own unique design altogether.

Some blogging platforms offer the ability to pay one flat rate for as many blogs as you'd like, which is something to consider. While you may start out thinking one blog is all you will have, trust me when I say that ideas for others will emerge, and you may like the idea of paying one flat rate for all your blogs.

Personally, I use Typepad and have since 2009. I have been happy with its blogging platform and haven't felt the need to make a switch. One area where I think that WordPress has Typepad beat is when it comes to the look of their templates. You can find a lot of nice templates that with WordPress, while you are more limited with Typepad. With Typepad, I pay one flat fee per year and can have as many blogs as I want, and have unlimited storage space. I've only had to contact their customer service over the years a couple of times, and they have always provided good support, too.

I have also used WordPress and Blogger. I have nothing against either of these blogging platforms; I just feel comfortable using Typepad, since I've been with them since 2009. While I liked the look and ease of use of the WordPress blog I worked on, which was hosted by Bluehost, I didn't care for all the plug-ins and how things could go wrong with them (and at times did, costing us money to hire tech support).

With Typepad, in comparison, you don't have all those plug-ins, and it provides the software and hosts the site. It is also a blog host that is geared more for the person who wants to blog who isn't tech-savvy. Having said that, I'm about to start another blog and I'm planning to go with WordPress so that I can have more options when it comes to the design, and I can get some more in-depth experience using the platform. Thus far, most of my experience using WordPress has come from posting what I write to client blogs.

No matter which blogging platform you choose, you should make sure that your blog will have responsive web design. People access websites using all different types of devices, such as desktop computers, phones, and tablets. Your website needs to respond to that device by making adjustments to the layout and look, so that it still looks good when accessed on something other than a desktop computer. Responsive web design ensures that the pages will show up looking up good, despite the type of device the person is using. If you plan to have a team of bloggers working on your blog, you will also want to select a host that allows for multiple writers.

HOW TO SET UP YOUR BLOG

When it comes to setting up your blog, the first steps are going to vary depending on which platform you use. You will also decide whether you will purchase the domain name through the blogging platform, if it offers that service, or if you will purchase it through a place like GoDaddy or Network Solutions. You can purchase your domain name through a place other than the blogging platform you choose to use. You will just need to map the domain and set it up to work with the blogging platform. While this sounds scary if you are not technical, it's really not. Blogging platforms have detailed instructions written up that explain step-by-step how you will set up and map your domain for using it with their service.

When you register your domain, whether on your own or with the blogging platform you will be using, be sure that you are the owner of it. If you are registering it on your own, you will be, but if you are registering it through a blogging platform, make sure you are the domain owner, and not the blogging platform company. That way you will own the domain name and can take your blog with you to other platforms, if you choose to do so.

Your first steps in setting up a blog are to explore the various blogging platforms and decide which one you will use. Then you will want to register your blog domain name, either with the blogging platform or outside of there. Once you have your domain name registered, you are ready to get started setting up the blog. Depending on which platform you use, there should be information that walks you through the setup process. You will choose a template and begin filling in the information you want on the blog. You can get started with adding information about what your blog is about, customizing areas, and writing your first posts.

If you choose a blog platform that provides you with the blogging software and the hosting services, you will just log in, select your template, and start customizing your blog. If you opt for one that is hosted separately, such as WordPress, you will need to also set up a hosting account with a company that will host your blog. You can choose any website hosting company that says it will host WordPress sites.

If you are new to blogging, it may seem overwhelming just to decide what platform to use to create your blog. It is an important decision to make, because it will influence the look of your blog and the ease of using the software, and if you end up not liking one platform, it may be a pain to move your blog to another one. However, the decision you make is not set in stone, so keep that in mind. Just because you choose one blogging platform now, it doesn't mean you can't move your blog to a different one later on. Don't think you will be making a fatal mistake if you choose the wrong blogging platform; you won't be doing that at all. It's never set in stone.

How comfortable you are with your technical skills is going to influence the platform you select and feel confident using. If you feel you have no technical skills, then you should consider getting started with a blogging platform that provides the software and hosting services, giving you everything you need at one site. If you feel you have some technical skills, or learning them doesn't scare you, then you may feel confident opting for a blogging platform where you have more customization options and can put your technical skills to use. In my opinion, a good option for those who don't feel they are tech-savvy and just want a simple route to blogging would be to use Typepad, while those who have some tech skills or feel comfortable learning them may want to opt for WordPress.

Before making a decision about which blogging platform you will use, log on to investigate a few of the options. Take a look at the templates that they have to offer, view some of the blogs that have been created using that platform—you may even want to set up a trial blog. Some platforms offer a two-week trial, giving you the chance to try out their software and see what you think. Deciding on the platform you will use doesn't have to be done in ten minutes. Take the time you feel you need in order to choose the one that you feel is right for you.

BLOGGER SPOTLIGHT
Bethany Spohr
All Natural Savings
www.allnaturalsavings.com

When did you first start blogging and what got you interested in doing so?
After several years of health issues, and finding natural ways to help alleviate my symptoms, I had a desire to start a blog to help others experiencing the same issues. My blog started as a way to share my natural health experiences, but as my readers shared feedback, saying they'd love to also live a natural lifestyle, but it was just too expensive for them, the idea for a natural savings blog was born. I changed my blog to a hub for organic coupons, deals, and natural savings tips, due to reader feedback, and it took off from there. Having that passion for helping others was key, along with listening to my readers' needs. That passion is what still drives me today.

What blogging format do you use, and are you happy with it?
I use WordPress for my blog. Overall I am happy with it. It is technical, so I have to hire out when I want to change my blog's look or if there are technical issues. The appearance and theme options of WordPress are very professional and there are so many hosts to choose from, which makes it affordable.

How long did it take before you were making a good salary each year from your blog?

I started making a few hundred dollars a month within the first year and after the second year I made a good part-time income, followed by a full-time income in my third year.

What did you find to be your biggest challenge in blogging, and how did you overcome it?

My biggest challenge is the tech side of it. While I love to blog and write, I just don't have the knowledge to code or design my site. Having a good tech person is key to running a blog, or self-training and taking classes, so that you can keep up with the tech side of the blog.

What advice would you offer to new bloggers, or those who are still struggling to earn money from their blog?

Providing good content is the most important thing, but getting people to find your content can be challenging. Offering free guest posts to top bloggers in your genre is a great way to get exposure and new readers to your blog. The more readers, the higher your income will be, as long as your blog has ads and affiliate links.

What is one thing you have done that has helped you be able to earn more blogging?

Analyzing my top income source and focusing 80 percent of my posts on that affiliate has been the most helpful.

What is your top tip for bloggers who want to earn a salary from their blog?

The more work you can put into it in the beginning, through guest posts, good content, and SEO (search engine optimization), the less work you'll have to do later to earn a salary. I put a lot more time into my blog in the beginning when I was building it, and now I can just focus on writing as I rank well with SEO and have a good reader base.

2

Keeping Your Blog Active

Once you get your blog set up, you will find that there is a little learning curve. You will need to learn the ins and outs of how to use the blogging platform software, how to make changes, and how to keep your blog running smoothly. One of the problems that many bloggers have is that they are filled with excitement to get the blog started, but after they do a couple of posts, they have lost their interest. There are many blogs that have been started and have gone absolutely nowhere.

Every once in a while I will stumble across someone's blog and read a post that I like, only to go to their home page and see that they haven't posted anything in a long time. Sometimes, years have gone by since their last post. You may have seen this as well. People who get their blog started, and then the posts begin to taper off until they eventually are only posting maybe once a while, with large spans of time between posts, or less or they are simply no longer posting at all.

There can be many reasons as to why blogs die. Some people may lose interest in the topic, change their goals, or lose ideas to write about. There are some bloggers who start many different kinds of blogs only to see which ones have traction and which ones don't. Then they ax the blogs that they don't feel are going to go anywhere, and turn their focus to blogs that are doing well or show a lot of promise. Let me warn you now that blogging is contagious. Many people start that first blog learning how to do it, only to then go on to start numerous others. Each time you start a new one, it becomes easier, but then you will need to determine if you are going to keep it active or let it become another lost site in the blogosphere.

WHY KEEPING IT ACTIVE MATTERS

If you want to make money from your blogging, it is important that you keep it active. Once you start writing blog posts, you will have fresh content and stale content. The stale content is the posts that will become old and outdated. The fresh content is the new posts that you publish. If you continue to put out fresh content on your blog, you will end up ranking higher in search engines. The search engines, such as Google, need to continuously serve up relevant, fresh content to those doing searches on them. If they do, they will continue to be trusted and be seen as doing their job. If they were to keep serving up all outdated and stale content, then people would grow tired of that.

Ask yourself, if you were searching around for a specific topic, would you prefer to read a blog post that was written within the last few months, or would you want one that was from years ago? Unless you are specifically searching for something history-related, you will most likely want fresh, newer content to read, and that's the same for other people, too. Blogs that are updated regularly are going to end up being ranked higher and get served up higher within search engines.

Search engines have been programmed to be able to tell if sites are being updated regularly or if they have become stagnant. Those sites that are idle and not being updated will tend to lose traffic after a while because the search engine will instead serve up sites that are putting out fresh content.

Even if you have a lot of friends and family, you will still need to rely on search engines to bring a lot of traffic to your blog. Therefore you have to do things that will help make your blog more attractive to search engines, so they continuously put your site in the results when people do searches. Around 80 percent of the traffic to my blogs comes directly from search engines.

Keeping your blog active is not only for search engine purposes, but also for your readers. If you are to grow an audience of people who enjoy your blog, you will need to keep providing them with content (or videos) or they will tend to forget about you and your blog. It's kind of like the old saying, "out of sight, out of mind." They need to keep hearing from you or they will probably be reading someone else's blog instead. That doesn't mean that you have to be fixated on posting constantly, but it does mean that you need to have some regularity. Your regularity may be once a month, and that's okay, but whatever it is you are comfortable with, you have to stick with it to keep your blog active.

If you are reading this and you are a blogger who has stagnant blogs that you had given up on, you may be having second thoughts about them at this point. It's never too late to go back and resurrect that blog and continue on. You will want to have a plan for what you are going to do to bring it back, in terms of sprucing up the design, adding fresh content, and letting any social media followers know that you are back. You can even do a blog post on the fact that you are back and what your vision is moving forward.

Having said all that, you may end up being a blogger who starts many blogs and sees what works and what doesn't. I have started more blogs than I currently continue. I have had ideas for blogs and started them, only to a year or two later lose interest in the topic or feel that it's not worth putting in more time. I have some favorite blogs that seem to get most of my attention, and don't feel all that bad letting the others go. You need to see what works and what you feel is worth putting more time into.

ACTIVE GOALS

If you are going to have a blog that you make money from, you will have to make it a priority to keep it active. This means you will need to publish on it with regularity. If you are serious about making money from blogging, then you have to be serious about publishing posts. It's about making the commitment. Success doesn't usually come overnight. A blog is something you will create and then continuously work at growing and improving.

I have numerous blogs, including *Volusia County Moms*. It's a local blog that targets one county in the entire country. I started it in 2009, and at the time, it was just something I worked on as a side project. I didn't realize at the time that I could make some money from blogging, so it was something I was doing for fun on the side as a writer. For the first two years that I had the blog, I never made any money from it. I didn't try to, and the thought hadn't crossed my mind. Then one day out of the blue, a local business contacted me and said they would love to advertise on the blog. A light bulb went off. I realized at this moment that I had something with earnings potential. That's when I began taking the blog more seriously and seeing it as a way to earn money. It wasn't long after that point when I had a hundred advertisers on the blog. While I had never let the blog sit stagnant during those two first years, seeing that I could earn money from the blog lit a fire under me, and I began posting more often.

There is no magic number when it comes to how many blog posts you should write per day, week, or month. It depends on the type of blog you have, the amount of time you can give, and your target market. If you are writing in-depth science blog posts, for example, then publishing one per week would likely be sufficient. If, on the other hand, you are posting about the best grocery deals, you will need to publish more often than that. Every blog is different, so you will need to find a happy balance that works for you and your blog. At the very minimum, no matter what type of blog you have, you should try to publish a post once a week. That will keep the blog fresh and continue to keep offering content. It stands to reason that the more you post, the more traffic you are likely going to get, assuming your posts are of interest to people and you have written them in a manner that will get them noticed.

What is more important than the quantity of posts is the quality of your posts. It's important that you are publishing something that people will want to read or see. Rather than just trying to get as many posts as possible, aim for content that is going to be of interest to your target market. That is going to matter more in the long run than how many posts you have done. Quality content is always going to win over quantity. If what you are publishing is deemed low quality or not of use to your target market, then it won't matter how many posts you publish. If you publish things that your readers find interesting, helpful, or entertaining, they will want to continue coming back to your blog. They will also want to share those posts with others, which will bring more people to your site.

Some people will set up a schedule to help hold themselves accountable as to how often they will publish a blog post. Others will just kind of wing it and publish posts when they feel the inspiration. There is no right or wrong way to do it. You can do whatever method works for you, as long as you keep your blog active. If you have a day job, you may find that it works out best for you to write a new post every Saturday morning while everyone else is still in bed. You may be someone who finds they can write three blog posts every Sunday, and then schedule them to automatically publish on different days throughout the week.

Each scenario is fine; it's just a matter of what works for you in your life.

The bottom line is that if you want to be a blogger, you have to make the time to blog. Even if you dedicate yourself to spending twenty minutes per day on your blog, commit to writing a certain number of posts per week, or decide the last thing you will do before bed each night is blog, you have to put in the time. Your blog will not go anywhere if you don't put in the effort to keep it active and growing. If you do put in the time and effort, you will see it grow and get traffic. With some dedication and patience, you should see good things happen.

One way to maintain an active blog if you do not want to be the one to do all the blogging is to have guest bloggers and others who are contributors. If you start a blog on entertainment news, for example, you don't have to be the only person who writes about everything that is going on in the world of entertainment. You can have a team of bloggers who all contribute to the blog with their own posts. With two or more people contributing to the blog, there is a good chance it's going to remain active. If this idea interests you, just be sure to go with a blogging platform that allows for multiple bloggers. Each of you can have a login and contribute posts. You can also accept guest posts from others who would like to contribute to your blog, which is something we will discuss more in the next chapter.

BLOG POST IDEAS

As a writer, I'm someone who sees ideas everywhere. I could come up with ten ideas for blog posts within a minute. It comes easily for me because I see ideas for content in everything. But I have come to realize that it doesn't come that easily for most people. This is probably one of the reasons that some blogs go stagnant or die completely. Many people run out of ideas to blog about, or they feel they are stuck without being able to come up with more to say that is somewhat related to the nature of their blog.

I suggest keeping a little notebook where you can write down blog post ideas. Keep a running list so that you can refer back to it anytime you need a topic to write about. Choose a notebook that has a pocket, so you can add ideas to it that you come across. You never know what items you may stick in there that can inspire blog post ideas later on. Everything from the fortune you get in your cookie to pieces of junk mail that come to the house may end up at some point becoming a blog post idea. Add interesting items to your notebook folder for later consideration. I keep a notebook like this and add ideas to it often. Some of the ideas may never become blog posts, but it's a good way to brainstorm ideas, so that you have some options later on when you need something to blog about.

Your blog post ideas can include your own personal experiences, thoughts, goals, reviews, and more. There's no limit to what you can or should write about on your blog, as long as you are somewhat keeping it related to the theme of your blog and it would be of interest to your target market. I have had a vegetarian blog since 2009. There are many different angles I have taken on there, including posting recipes, product reviews, random musings, research articles, and more. I have more ideas for blog posts than I have time to write. That's a good position to be in. But I didn't just get lucky; I see ideas everywhere.

There are many ways you can obtain ideas for things to write about. Here are a few ways to try to drum up ideas.

Google Trends

Google offers what is called Google Trends, which is a tool you can use to see what people are searching for. When you go to the site, you can type a term or topic into the search box, and it will show you if there are a lot of people searching for those topics. You can use this to get ideas of things to blog about. Let's say you have a blog that covers Florida theme parks. You can type that term into the search tool and get a list of things that people are searching for that are related to that term. You will also be given breakout topics that are offshoots of that main topic, but still tend to relate. Click around on the ideas and write some of them down. These are the things that people are searching for that are related to your blog topic.

Make a habit of logging onto Google Trends once a week and searching to see what people are looking for. Let's say you have a blog that is all about pets. You cover pet care, nutrition, travel, sitting, and more. Be sure to type each one of those areas into Google Trends to see what type of ideas you can get for new blog posts. These topics are current trends that are being searched for, so you will want to use the ideas sooner rather than later. Google Trends can be a wonderful tool for bloggers because you can see how popular a topic is, as well as get ideas that you can blog about.

Scanning the News

The news can be a great source of blog post ideas because you may see something being covered you hadn't thought of, you may want to counter something you read, or you may want to expand on an angle that was covered in the news. I like to go to Google News once a day and scan the headlines. You can also create favorite topics that they will compile for you. Take a few minutes to look through the headlines, read a few articles, and see if it inspires any blog post ideas. You can also do a search on Google News once every few days or so to see what is being covered on your topic area. You may find articles you want to piggyback on. There's absolutely nothing wrong with stealing an article idea, so long as you don't steal the author's work. There's nothing illegal about taking the topic someone else wrote about and writing your own unique blog post on the same topic. Use the news to generate some ideas for your blog posts. Likewise, you can search around on Google's search engine to get ideas, too.

Use Social Media

Going on social media can be a good source of blog post ideas. See what people are posting, read a few of the comments, check out the memes. All of it can be inspiration for blog post topics. Also, there are social media groups that can be helpful in drumming up ideas. Facebook, for example, has groups you can join for just about everything. Find a group or two related to your blog topic and then join it. Not only will you be able to get blog post ideas from it, but you will be able to promote your blog there as well, by posting links to your blog posts that relate to what is being discussed. You can also read the comments on your blog posts and other bloggers' posts to get ideas.

Consider Your Analytics

In a later chapter, you will you learn about using analytics on your blog, which will show you the most popular pages on your site, among other things. You can use your analytics to get blog post ideas, too. Take a look at what is popular on your blog and then do more of those kinds of posts. If you see that reviews are popular, do more reviews. If you see that coupon posts are popular, offer up more of those. If tips articles are bringing in the traffic, then you will want to do more tips articles. You can also see what is popular and do a spin-off from those older articles, taking a fresh twist or expanding on the topic.

Look to Others

There are ways you can get blog post ideas by looking to others for help. There are numerous ways you can do this, including asking your readers what they want to read about or if they have questions. You can also interview others who are a part of the topic you are covering. If you have a blog that is all about taking cruises, you could interview an expert for cruise tips for families who may have special-needs children. Get creative and get others involved if you need some ideas and if you want to add another layer of interesting content to your blog.

Find Some Facts

Research can help generate some blog post ideas that are not only relevant, but timely. Many bloggers can find great ideas by checking out the latest research that is out on PubMed. The National Institutes of Health website offers up information on the latest peer-reviewed research that has been conducted around the world. Most of the time, you will be able to read the research recaps, which give you the gist of the research conducted and the results. Sometimes you can access the full articles, but as long as you have the standard recap, you are good to go. You can use that information for blog post ideas. For example, if you have a blog that covers arthritis, you can log on to this site every month and conduct a search for the term. The results will produce a list of all the recent published research on that topic.

You should be able to find some that fit the theme of your blog, and you can use the study as an article or reference it in a larger piece. Additionally, you can scour places like the Pew Research Center for statistics and polls that may relate to your topic. There is always research and statistics that can be found and used on your blog. Just be sure when writing the article to cite where you got the information from.

Get Outside

If you are someone who likes to get outdoors for some fresh air, you know how inspiring it can be. Taking a walk outside, sitting in the park, or going for a hike can do a lot to help boost your creativity. If you feel like you can't think of blog post ideas, take a walk outside. The brain-boosting power of nature will get your creative juices flowing, and you will likely come back feeling energized and with at least one idea to get writing about.

There are many ideas all around you, and the more you start recognizing them and writing them down, the better you will be at picking them out. With a little practice at it, you will be able to quickly come up with a variety of topics to write about, so that you never run out of fresh content on your blog.

BLOGGING FOR OTHERS

In addition to blogging for my own blogs, I write blog posts for numerous other people's blogs. There are many people who want to have a blog, yet they may not have the time to put into writing the posts for one. This is true of businesses, doctors, and others who see the marketing value in having a blog, but don't have the time or interest in being the one to write the posts for it.

This is a good thing for you because if you are interested in doing some ghost blogging for someone, which is where you will do the writing of each post but won't get credit for it, you can earn money from your blogging skills.

I have been writing blog posts for other people's blogs for years. I have regular clients whom I write for each month and it's an ongoing thing. If you get blogging jobs like this, you may be asked to log into their blogging account and do the posting of each article, or you may be asked to write up the blog posts and just submit them and they will handle the posting of them. Either way, you will earn money from each post that you write. In such cases, I typically recommend that the person or business post at least once per week. They will usually have me write four or more blog posts at once, and they will schedule them out to publish as often as they see fit.

If you blog for others, you will want to know the importance of keeping their blog active, so you can continue to drive traffic to their site. They may ask you to come up with the blog post ideas, they may supply you with the ideas, or you may have a combination of the two routes to having topics. If you are ghost blogging for others, you can use the same methods listed above to come up with a list of topics to blog about.

The beauty in being a blogger is that you can make money from running your own blogs, but it's also a service you can offer to others. Many companies would like to have a blog, but don't have the staff to dedicate to it. They will, however, outsource something like this to a freelancer, which will give you an additional income stream as you are caring for your own blogs.

BLOGGER SPOTLIGHT
Maurie Lung
Muddy Boots Adventures
www.muddybootsadventures.net

When did you first start blogging and what got you interested in doing so?

I first started blogging in 2016, officially creating its own website in early 2017, after repeated requests from people to share my stories with a broader audience. When I became a mother, I never expected how profoundly and painfully my heart could ache. And to be fair, nor did I clearly fathom how deeply joyful the love I also experience would be. I did expect difficult conversations and having to make decisions about how to teach and model and practice values that are important to me. I started to share these stories of these unexpected and sometimes challenging experiences with my children in private conversations with my friends, then more openly on my Facebook, and finally, I leapt into a very public arena of blogging.

What blogging format do you use, and are you happy with it?

I use WordPress and I have been surprised at how user-friendly it is, especially for a technology dinosaur like me.

How long did it take before you were making a good salary each year from your blog?

I was surprised at how quickly I was able to make money from my blog and how it came in different forms, such as advertising, content sharing, or facilitating workshops. My blog is not my primary income; however, I met my income goal within a year.

What did you find to be your biggest challenge in blogging, and how did you overcome it?

My biggest challenge in blogging is consistency. One of the ways that I found particularly helpful is to write several blog posts and then schedule their release, versus writing and posting immediately. Another practice that was particularly helpful was to schedule a block of time on my calendar to write and to write in a setting that supported the ideal writing environment for me, which is quiet and without distractions. Finally, I started making mini-notes on my calendar about ideas for writing so that when I sit down to write, I have been primed for the post.

What advice would you offer to new bloggers, or those who are still struggling to earn money from their blog?

My best advice is to write about what interests you, your passions and your values. Focus on relevant content will inform how you need to present it and who can benefit from connecting to it.

What is one thing you have done that has helped you be able to earn more blogging?

Changing my thinking to use my blog as a content marketing tool that drives clients to my business was the biggest thing that helped me earn more from the blogging.

What is your top tip for bloggers who want to earn a salary from their blog?

After strong content, the next priority is to build sincere relationships through connecting on social media, forums, and other networking opportunities so that people know that your blog exists!

3

All About Writing

Unless you are going to have a blog that focuses on videos—a vlog—you will need to hone your writing skills. Many people may wonder if they can make money as a blogger if they are not also a professional writer. Having great writing abilities is wonderful, because it helps you to have a blog that will help you put forth a great image. If you feel that you are at least a decent writer, you should be able to manage writing blog posts. Don't let the fear of writing keep you away from blogging. Rather, learn some tips and tools of the trade to become a better writer. As with anything else in life, the more you do it, the better you are likely to become. You can improve your writing skills with effort.

For me, I was a writer before I became a blogger, so blogging became a natural extension to my writing. When I was a college student at the University of Nevada Las Vegas (UNLV), I saw an ad in the student newspaper that they were hiring news writers. I was immediately interested and applied. My whole life I had loved writing, and people told me that I was a good writer, but for some reason it hadn't clicked with me that I could actually make a living at it. I have no idea why, but it hadn't crossed my mind that I could become a professional writer.

Becoming a news writer for the UNLV student newspaper was my first step toward my writing career. From there, I took a course on campus in news writing, and began moving in the direction to enter the field. I went on to become a full freelance writer in 2004, and haven't looked back since. It was the perfect fit for me. I have made my living every year by freelance writing. It was in 2009 that I started my first blogs, and even then I didn't realize that I could make money doing so. I started the blogs for my own personal reasons. One was a hobby, and the other was me solving a problem that I thought my community had. Two years into blogging, I started making money from my blogs and realized that you can earn a living from blogging.

When I realized how lucrative blogging could be, I amped up what I was doing, created more blogs, and made it a larger part of my overall career. These days, half of my income each year comes from blogging, and half of it comes from freelance writing. I'm not willing to give up the time put into either of the areas, because I love them both, and I appreciate that my income is diversified, not relying on one or the other. However, if I ever did want to give up my freelance writing side, I have complete confidence that income would be replaced by blogging. Still, I love the balance of both areas, and love the variety that it provides to my life. I love freelance writing and I love blogging, and for me, they both merge together to create a wonderful and satisfying career.

No matter what type of field you are in, you can enter the field of blogging. There are people who blog who come from all different walks of life. They have a multitude of experiences, and their writing skills vary. The great thing about blogging for bucks it that you don't have to have a certain skill set or any particular experience in order to start doing it and be successful at it. Blogging is a fairly new area of the career world, providing everyone with an equal opportunity to jump in, share what they know or want to focus on, and earn a living from it. While it doesn't matter what area or background you come to blogging from, you may still find it helpful to have a few tips on writing blog posts.

WRITING TIPS

If you are not someone who is a writer, you may have a little anxiety about blogging. Let me first say that there are many blogs that do more videos than written content. They are called vlogs, which are video blogs, and they are done by vloggers. If you have interest in doing that, you can make videos and post them to your blog, but you should still have a little written content to go with it for search engine purposes. However, many people will want to focus more on blog posts that offer written content. Don't let the fact that you are not a writer scare you away from writing blog posts.

I had been a freelance writer for several years before I ever started my first blog. Therefore, writing blog posts was an easy extension of what I had already been doing, which was writing articles for magazines and newspapers. Whether you have experience writing articles or you are just getting into it, don't worry. With some practice you should become more comfortable with it. It's important to understand that there are no hard-and-fast rules when it comes to writing blog posts. You have a lot of room for doing what you want with your blog posts. Even so, there are many questions that people have when it comes to writing blog posts.

One of the questions many have regarding blog posts is the ideal length. Well, there is no ideal length for a blog post that you need to follow. I've written and read some that are short, and I've also done the same with some that are quite long. Typically speaking, I would say to aim for a blog post that is at least three hundred to four hundred words in length if you are writing content. I have a blog where I post a lot of local events that are going on, and then link them to an events calendar. The posts are often flyers for the events, and I do not write a lot of content to go with them. When people send me the flyers, they will sometimes include some content to go with it, but not always. I do like to make sure I have some content there for search engine purposes, so on something like that, I will just write a couple of lines with a recap of the information from the flyer. However, if I'm writing a blog post on a specific topic and sharing my thoughts or information on the subject, then I'll try to make sure I have at least three hundred to four hundred words for the post.

Chances are you read articles online, too. Have you ever noticed the type of article that you prefer to read? Keep that in mind when it comes to writing your own posts. What catches your eye and keeps you reading, or quickly provides you with the info you are looking for, is something you likely share with many others. We live in busy times, and people don't always like to spend a lot of time reading lengthy articles, but they still want the information. There has been research done to see what people look at when they log on to your site. Truth be told, a lot of the time people merely skim articles, rather than read them in their entirety. There are some articles I read completely, but I'm also one of those who skim some articles, as well.

Following are some tips to keep in mind when it comes to writing your blog posts.

Search Engine Optimization (SEO) Counts

Blog posts need to be written with some SEO mixed in. The easiest way to understand SEO is to think in terms of how your potential reader would think. What would they type into the search bar in order to find your article or blog? You want to sprinkle some of those keywords into your blog post to help the search engines be able to match your article to what people are searching for, and then offer it in the search results. If you are targeting a local area, for example, you need to make sure you use your city name or geographic area in your writing. If you have a whole blog that is targeting people in the Chicago area, yet your posts never mention the word *Chicago*, you are going to miss out on a lot of traffic.

Don't overdo it on the keywords, which is known as keyword stuffing, and don't use them in a way that doesn't sound natural when the line is being read. Keywords should be sprinkled in and used in a way that sounds natural and blends in with the writing. I have a fellow successful blogger friend that has a theory that if you want your blog to dominate in a particular area, you should choose three keywords and use those same three keywords in every blog post that you write.

Create Good Headlines

An extension of using SEO wisely, it's important that your posts have good headlines in order to attract readers and help search engines locate your blog. The headlines should be compelling enough to make the reader want to click on the link to see what the article has to say. Focus on creating simple, short titles that compel people to want to read the post. This takes some practice, so don't worry if you find it difficult at first. You will get the hang of it the more headlines you create.

Having said that, I would advise avoiding what is referred to as clickbait. When you engage in clickbait, you are creating a headline that is sensationalist and merely for the purpose of getting the person to click on the link. Oftentimes, clickbait headlines seem outrageous, which is what draws people into clicking on the link, only to be disappointed by what the content really is on the page. While clickbait may draw people to the blog by getting them to click on the outlandish headline, it's not likely to build a loyal readership. People will come to know that the blog focuses on clickbait, and they will tend to ignore it once they catch on.

Write for the Reader

As we have established, many people prefer to skim articles for the info, rather than take the time to read the entire post. One way to help make your posts more reader-friendly is to use bullet points, with each point offering information. You could also use subheadings throughout the article, and you could even have a recap section. Many websites today offer a recap of the article, with the most important pieces of information being pulled out and listed in the recap.

The recap can be found at the beginning of the article, so the person gets the information, even if they don't continue to read on. This isn't a practice I use, but I have seen others use it. I do, however, like to use bullet point lists in my posts so that they are more reader-friendly. Many people who are in a hurry will still take the time to scan your bullet point list for useful information. It's a good idea in longer blog posts to also use some subheadings in order to break up the information, make it look more appealing, add to the flow of the article, and help with search engine traffic.

Add Links

Search engines like that you offer links to credible information in your posts. If you are writing about a research article, for example, add in the link to the research article page, so users can check it out if they want to. You would do this by linking the actual words (e.g., "According to the Centers for Disease Control and Prevention") and having it open to a new window. You don't want to overload your blog posts with links, of course, but adding in a few here or there is a good thing.

Share Your Personality

One of the beautiful things about being a blogger is that you get to share your personality with readers. It's good for them to get to know some of what your personality is like, so don't be afraid to share that with them. Your blog posts don't need to be all professional, cold, and mechanical. When bloggers let their personality shine, they are more likely to make a connection with the readers and build a loyal fan base.

Know Where You Are Going

Some people can sit down and just start writing a blog post with very little thought prior to the first words being typed onto the screen. Most people, however, would benefit from having a blueprint of where they are going with the post. For some posts it may make sense to simply write and go where it takes you. For other posts, you may want to jot down a quick outline of your thoughts and what you want to cover. This is something I have always done for posts that are more in-depth or lengthier. I make a simple outline so I know what I'll cover in the opening paragraph, in the bullet points, and in the closing. I'll make a list of any specific facts or details that I want to include in the piece. Doing this just helps you gather your thoughts and makes it easier to work your way through the post.

Add an Image

Most bloggers add at least one image to their blog post. If you have images to use, that is great. If you need some, you can buy images from stock photo sites, and you can use Canva to create your own images. I love Canva and use it to create a lot of images for my blogs. Many bloggers add an image alt attribute, which may help with search engine results.

Evergreen Topics

Many of the blog posts you write will be about what is going on in the here and now. Whether you are covering a current issue in the news or culture or you are reviewing a new product or movie, it's something that is of interest to the audience right now. In addition to those topics, you may want to include some blog posts that cover what are considered to be evergreen topics.

These are topics that are going to always be relevant to the readers. Five years from now, they will still be interested in reading about that one thing, whatever it may be. I have a nature blog where I blog about hikes my family and I have taken around Florida. The trails remain the same year after year, so those posts are evergreen. People can read those posts for years, and they are still relevant. The same goes for the many blog posts I've done on the natural springs in the state. This gives your blog a layer of depth that will keep people reading those posts, as well as your new ones.

These are just some tips to keep in mind when it comes to the writing. You can pick and choose what works for you. Over time you will develop your own style and become comfortable with how you want your blog posts to be. It's also a good idea to take a look at some other blogs to see what you like and don't like about how they write their blog posts. Spend an hour randomly pulling up blog posts online, on a variety of topics, to see how bloggers formulate their posts. This will give you some ideas about what you would like to include, what you would like to avoid, and so on.

GRAMMAR AND SPELL-CHECKING

I've seen blog posts that are written with perfect grammar, and I've seen ones that are anything but. As I mentioned above, there's a lot of room for creativity and making the blog style your own. I don't spend a lot of time worrying about grammar, but I do read it over and try to pick out any glaring errors or misspelled words. Let me be the first one to say that it is difficult to find your own errors in any writing that you do.

In my first year of being a freelance writer, I would spend a lot of time combing over my newspaper and magazine articles prior to sending them into the editor. I would try so hard to find any errors, to avoid there being even one little letter out of place. Lo and behold, it didn't matter how much time I spent combing over the piece after I wrote it. I would always find out that there was one little error here or there once it was in the editor's hands. I became frustrated, wondering why it was that I was missing these things, despite the effort I was making to not miss them.

I spent a little time researching the issue, trying to find the solution to the problem. What I found out from my research from credible sources was that it's extremely difficult to find the errors in your own writing. This is because your brain tends to read over it as you intended, rather than as you actually wrote it. Your brain quickly takes misspelled words and deciphers what it was supposed to be, so you read it correctly.

Once I had this revelation, I decided to stop spending so much time proofreading my work, and I hired a proofreader. Since 2005, I have had a proofreader who goes over all of my paid writing work prior to my sending it into my client. The person is just another pair of eyes that is going over the work, looking for any of those little errors that my brain simply can't spot because I wrote it. When someone else reads what you wrote, they are in a better position to catch your errors, because they are reading it for the first time. They don't have any preconceived ideas about your message, and their brain is more alert to errors.

For my own personal blogs, I don't usually pay to have the proofreader go over those. I go over it myself and then post it. There are times later when I may spot an error I didn't see when I first posted it. If that happens, I just edit the post to fix it and move on. No big deal. However, I do a lot of ghostwriting for other people's blogs, and I do pay to have each of those blog posts proofread before sending them to my client.

The bottom line is that you want to have perfectly written posts; we all do. But we are also all human and subject to minor errors. It happens. Fix it where you can, try to avoid them as much as you can, but don't obsess over them or let the fear of mistakes keep you from marching on. Once you write a post you should spell-check it, read it over, and maybe even let it sit for a little bit before going back over it one more time and then posting. Blog posts are not set in stone or published in a newspaper, book, or magazine. You can easily go back and edit any errors that are spotted later.

BLOGGING FOR CORPORATIONS

Many businesses have a blog, because it's a great marketing tool. They may have an employee who writes their blog posts, or they may outsource the work. Many businesses choose to outsource their blog post writing to ghostwriters. As a ghostwriter, which is something I do a lot of, you won't get the credit for the work you are doing, but you do get the income. I do blog post writing for numerous companies on a regular basis. There are some I have been writing blogs for over the course of five years or more. It's a steady supply of work and income, as well as something I enjoy doing. You may find that you enjoy blogging for others as well. Blogging for others is discussed in depth in chapter 11.

Whether you are writing blog posts for your own blogs or decide to branch out and take on writing for some companies that have blogs, you can earn a lot of money from blogging. When you decide to combine the two income streams, it can help keep you a busy blogger who has a steady supply of work, and you will keep the work varied. Some people may not appreciate that, but I personally love being able to write on a wide variety of topics. Being a generalist, I'm always learning about new things, because I get a chance to research and write about new things on a weekly basis. It never gets dull or boring. Rather, it continuously keeps me interested and engaged, and finds me new things to discover.

BLOGGER SPOTLIGHT

Caroline Eubanks
This Is My South
www.thisismysouth.com

When did you first start blogging and what got you interested in doing so?
I started blogging back in high school but didn't take it seriously until 2009. I'd read travel blogs and thought I could do the same.

What blogging format do you use, and are you happy with it?
I am on a self-hosted WordPress website and am very pleased with it. Since I learned how to manage it, it's been smooth sailing.

How long did it take before you were making a good salary each year from your blog?

I still don't have a "good salary" as I also work as a freelance writer, but my website started to cover costs and earn a profit in the last few years.

What did you find to be your biggest challenge in blogging, and how did you overcome it?

The hardest thing for me is doing it all. I currently manage most of the posts, photography, social media, and SEO. I hired someone to handle website maintenance, so that took a bit of pressure off.

What advice would you offer to new bloggers, or those who are still struggling to earn money from their blog?

Focus on SEO first. Content is great, but it doesn't really matter if it's not something people are interested in reading or can't find. That will help with everything else like ad sales and affiliate links.

What is one thing you have done that has helped you be able to earn more blogging?

I joined Mediavine ad network this year and it's been a total game changer. I now earn a comfortable amount.

What is your top tip for bloggers who want to earn a salary from their blog?

Hire someone to do what you're not good at. You don't actually have to do it all.

4

Ways to Promote Your Blog

Once you have your blog up and running and populated with posts, you will need to get some traffic to it. There are many ways that you can promote your blog. You don't have to engage in all of them. It's more important that you find the ones that work for you and that you don't mind doing. Promoting your blog can at times take as much time as writing the posts if you choose time-consuming routes. While this chapter will cover numerous ways to promote your blog, you don't have to do them all.

After reviewing the different ways you can promote your blog, you can then try a few out and see which ones you like. There will be some that you find more time-consuming and then others that seem quick and easy. Repeat the ones that work for you and ax the ones that seem like they weren't worth the effort. I have included a range of ways that you can promote your blog so that you have options, but I personally don't use all these methods. There are bloggers who do use the methods that I don't use.

MY PROMOTIONAL METHODS

I'm a firm believer that you should put most of your efforts into the blog, rather than into the various ways of promoting it. I know this may seem strange to some people, but that is what has worked for me. I believe if you put the time into your blog, it's going to go a long way toward bringing more people to the site. By this, I mean taking the time to produce blog posts that people will want to read, offering information they can use, and populating the blog with the right SEO keywords. When you do those things, you are automatically going to get more traffic to the site.

Even with putting my attention and time into the blog more than other promotional methods, I do still engage in a few other things to help promote my blogs. For one of my blogs, I have had a Facebook page for it for the last ten years. I use that page to post the links to the blog posts, and the main purpose of the page is to drive traffic to the blog. I have around 33,000 followers on that page, which is not bad because the focus is on one small county in the country. Still, analytics show that 80 percent of my traffic to that blog comes from searches, not from social media.

I promote one of my other blogs largely through Facebook groups. It's a vegetarian blog, and therefore I joined numerous online vegetarian and vegan groups. Some of the groups have more than a hundred thousand people in them. Every once in a while I will post a link to one of my blog posts in the group, but most of the time I comment on what others have posted about. People will ask a question or be looking for something that is fitting to a blog post of mine. Therefore, I comment by offering the link to the page that is a good fit. This route works well to drive a lot of traffic to the blog each month.

You have to be careful to not be overly spammy in doing this. You want to make sure that the links you are posting to your blog fit what is being discussed and that it makes sense to offer up that post. For example, I have a blog post that is a list of all family-friendly vegan recipes. Each of the recipes listed are linked to the recipe on my blog. If someone posts a question looking for recipes, I will post that one blog post link. From there, they may look at one page, or they may look at a dozen.

I dabble a bit in promoting my blogs in other places as well, such as on Instagram, but overall I don't do much to promote them outside of Facebook. I prefer to stick to focusing my efforts on the blog itself and then doing a little on the side to drive links and traffic to it.

KNOW YOUR TARGET MARKET

When it comes to being active in promoting your blog, it's important to know who your target market is. That's the only way you will know how to go about reaching them. Those who know marketing always identify their target market before putting forth the efforts to start engaging in promotion. So the first question you want to ask yourself is who your target market is. Who is the ideal person who would be interested in your blog? What is an average reader of your blog like? When you know the answers to those questions, you are more likely going to be able to narrow down where to find those people.

For example, with my vegetarian blog, I know that the people who would read that blog are going to be vegetarian or vegan, or may be curious about the lifestyle. By being able to identify that, I can use the information to know what type of groups I can join where I can promote my blog posts. That one may seem more straightforward than some people's blog themes. Let's say you have a blog focusing on personal training. You'd want to find people who are looking to lose weight and get healthy. It would be smart to join Facebook groups that focus on weight loss, exercising, and health. If you have a blog about dogs, join groups where dog lovers would be. If you have a blog about the laws of attraction, join groups that are focused on spiritual living, gratitude, and others that are fitting to that lifestyle.

What if you look for groups that fit your blog theme and you can't find any? If that happens, then create the group yourself. Having a Facebook group is free, and it's easy to create. Anyone can start one, and chances are there are plenty of other people who would join it. There are Facebook pages and Facebook groups, and both can help you promote your blog. The page focuses on promoting your blog name, while the group is made up of many people posting on a particular theme, and you can comment to promote your blog posts. Both can be helpful in terms of blog promotion. I will say, however, that if you spend too much time on these things it can be a disadvantage. This is where I say that the time is better spent working on your blog. There is a downside to using these routes to blog promotion.

The downsides that you can come across when using social media sites to promote your blogs do exist; however, few bloggers I've talked to seem to realize them. Most bloggers I know put a lot of effort into things like their Facebook pages. When I mention to them my concerns about doing that, it seems to make sense to them, and hopefully they back off a little and put that time and effort directly into the blog itself.

When you have a Facebook page to promote your blog (or any social media outlet), it's all short-lived. When you post something to Facebook, the algorithms are set to where only a small percentage of your followers actually see the post. This is purposeful, because Facebook wants you to spend money to reach those visitors. Well, most bloggers can't afford to boost every post, hoping that their followers will click on the link. That's just not a realistic goal. So even though you may have fifty thousand followers on your page, there may only be eight hundred who see your post. Don't get caught up thinking that all of your followers will see what you post and therefore you need to spend a lot of time on that page, because they won't and you shouldn't. Ideally, you should schedule the links to post, taking minutes to do so, and then leave the page and go work on your blog instead.

Another problem with using something like a Facebook page to promote your blog is that you don't own the page. You own your blog, but you don't own the Facebook page. Facebook owns that. And at any time they can change the rules, close your account, and do whatever they want, making it so you no longer have access to your page or the things you have posted. It's happened to many people before, even those who have had over a million followers.

Your goal should be to get the traffic and viewers to your site, not to your Facebook page. If you have a video to post on how to do something, put it in a blog post and then post the link to the video. Don't post the video itself. When you post the video itself, you are missing out on the traffic it would have driven to your site for people to see the video. And this brings me to the next problem with using such social media sites for promotion.

Social media promotion is short-lived. It's there and then it's gone. It's pushed down quickly and the next thing comes along. It's buried and likely will never be seen again. But if you put that time into your blog instead, it will have a longer-lasting effect. It will remain on your blog and can be accessed later. It doesn't get lost or buried like it does on social media. When it comes to social media, everything is here and gone in a snap, including the links to your blog posts.

It's important to note also that social media is about being, well, social. The last thing your followers want is you just plugging away post after post to promote yourself. You can get away with that in groups, but if it's your own social media page you will have to do more. You will need to be social. Your followers will want more than to be hit with links to your site day after day. They will want interaction from you, which can include you responding to their comments, answering their questions, and giving them a chance to voice their opinions. If you post a link to your new blog post, do so with asking a question about the topic, so that they can weigh in, which will get them to be social.

If you have a lot of followers this can be come time-consuming, so you have to determine how much time you want to put into being social and building your social media audience (some of which may like your page but never visit your site). Only you will know if the trade-off of your time is worth the effort. At one point, I was getting around fifty messages per day to my Facebook page from followers, and it was extremely time-consuming. I had to make adjustments to stop that, so I could focus my efforts on my actual blogs and writing projects. Now, I get just a few per day, and it's much easier to manage. The page is still sending me the same percentage of traffic to the blog each month, even though I'm putting in less time on the page now.

VARIOUS WAYS TO PROMOTE YOUR BLOG

Consider each of these ways to promote your blog to see which ones interest you in trying them. Not all of them will appeal to you, and that's okay. Not all of them may work well for your blog either. It's all about finding out what does work for you and which ones you feel are worth the time it takes to do them.

Social Media

Facebook was discussed at length above, because it's the world's largest social media outlet. There are nearly 2.5 billion people in the world who use Facebook. But it's also important to note that every social media platform has particular demographics. Knowing that will help you find your target market if you plan to promote your blog on social media. Younger people by and large don't use Facebook, for example. It's mostly women who use Pinterest. If you want to use social media for promotion, determine your target market and then find out which social media platforms that demographic uses.

If you are targeting twenty-year-olds, for example, you wouldn't focus your efforts on using Facebook. Other popular social media platforms include Instagram, Twitter, YouTube, Snapchat, LinkedIn, Pinterest, WhatsApp, and many others. It's all about using the one where your target market is. For each social media outlet that you choose to use, you will need to get down the specifics of the best way to promote your blog on that outlet. Keep in mind the importance of good images on social media. You can use Canva to create your own images and graphics. The site is user-friendly and offers free and paid options.

RSS Feeds

These are easy to set up and can help ensure that your blog posts get in front of those who want to read them regularly. The reader would subscribe to your RSS feed, and then every time you post something, the post would end up in the subscriber's feed. RSS stands for "Really Simple Syndication," and it really is an easy way to promote your blog. Once you set it up there's nothing else you need to do, because it just does the work for you.

Newsletters and Emails

You can promote your blog through emails and newsletters by having the readers opt in to receiving those messages from you. Some people simply offer the email sign-ups without any incentive, and others offer something to entice more people to subscribe. They may offer something like a special report that relates to the topics covered on the blog. There are numerous services you can use to have your blog posts go out via email to your readers, including MailChimp. You can set it up to where your blog posts automatically get sent out to your readers, or you can manually log in and create an email newsletter to send to them. Depending on the service you use and the number of subscribers you have, there may be a fee for using this type of promotion.

One thing you want to be sure to do is track this type of promotional effort to see if it's bringing people to your site. If you send out a newsletter, for example, take a look a few days later to see how many people opened it and how many people clicked on the link to go to your blog. I know many people like to use newsletters and emails, but I'm not a huge fan of them for several reasons. For starters, our inboxes have become inundated with spam and other emails that we simply hit the "delete" key on and never open. Plus, many emails from bloggers are filtered right into the spam folder, so the person who signed up to receive your message never does. This is a problem even with those with a huge audience, such as Seth Godin, who has blogged about how emails from blogs are being treated as spam. It's important to know this so you know if your efforts (and money if you are paying for the service) are worth it, and so you are not discouraged when you see barely anyone opening your message.

Having said that, my open rate is around 25 percent of those that I send the email to, which is around average. My click-through rate is around 8 to 10 percent. To me, that's hard to justify the costs of using something like MailChimp, once you have exceeded the number of contacts you can have for free (which is two thousand). Once you exceed the two thousand free contacts it will cost a monthly fee to email those contacts. You will have to decide if you feel the fee is justified and worth the return on investment.

Guest Posts

Some bloggers hate them and others love them. I fall somewhere in between, being selective regarding them. One way that people promote their blog and get backlinks to their site is to write or post guest posts. If you are a blogger who is accepting guest posts, you would take posts from others and post them on your blog. They would of course come with a byline and bio, which will contain a link to the post author, or the link may be in the body of the article. If you are someone who is writing a guest post for someone else's site, you would write the article and include a bio that promotes your blog and links to it.

The key here is to find bloggers who will accept your guest post, and vice versa. As a blogger, I get many solicitations per week from individuals and companies who want to provide me with guest posts. While it may give me a little content (that I wasn't looking for in the first place), the main goal here is promoting their site and providing a link to their site. These external links are important in helping with getting the site ranked higher. If you do go this route, be selective about where you post guest blogs if you will write for others, and in which ones you post on your own. You may find another blogger that has similar content and you swap guest posts to give each other a boost.

You want to make sure that you are getting something out of the exchange, that the content is good and fitting for your site, and that it makes sense to make this type of arrangement. While it's okay to write a few guest posts to put on other people's blogs, it's not a good idea to spend a lot of time doing this. The time would be better spent writing good quality posts for your own blog.

Signatures and Profiles

Consider the numerous places where you have your profile online. Each one of those places is ideal for promoting your blog. This is one promotional tool that I use. Create a standard email signature that goes on the bottom of each email and be sure to include your blog link. Your social media profiles should all offer a link to your blog, too. This is a free way to promote your blog and will get it in front of numerous people. Whether it's on LinkedIn, Pinterest, Facebook, or other platforms, always include your blog post link.

Include Sharing Buttons

Ideally, it's great if each blog post has sharing buttons that make it easy for the reader to share the post on their social media channels. If they read something that they like, they may be inclined to post it. Seeing the social media buttons may also put the thought into their mind, increasing the number of people who opt to do it. There's no better promotion that you can get for your blog than when someone other than you is doing the promoting of it. You posting the links to your blog is good, but someone else posting the links to your blog is far better.

Of course there are other ways you can promote your blog as well. You can engage in paying for advertising, including using Google Ads or social media paid advertising. If you do this be sure to consider your target market in formulating your campaign, and be sure to follow up to see what the results were. The only way to know if your promotional efforts are worth the time and money you put into them is if you are looking at your return on investment. I've tested online advertising for my blogs. I've probably spent around $50 on Facebook ads in the last ten years to promote various posts, only to come to the conclusion that I don't think they are worth it for me. I have talked to others who feel the same way. It's enticing to try them, and it's not a bad idea to do so, but pay attention to see if it's worth the return on investment.

You can also become a guest speaker on topics that relate to your blog theme, and promote your blog to the audience. You can write and send out a press release about your blog when you celebrate milestones or have information to share. For example, if your blog covers healthy cooking, you can write a blog post to send to your local newspapers that offers tips for healthy cooking and include an original recipe. They may print it, and your blog will get promoted through their publication. I've also seen bloggers promote their blogs through giveaways, bookmarks, mugs, booths at events, and a variety of other ways.

While on the topic of getting the most out of your promotional efforts, it's important to consider the best times to engage in promoting your blog posts. If you know your target market, you may have an idea of the times that they are mostly online, or when they tend to check their email. Pay attention to the reports provided by the promotional sites you use, such as Facebook and MailChimp, which will show the times people engaged with your post. You may find that it's useless to post your link on your social media site at 9:00 a.m., but if you post it at 7:00 p.m. it works to bring you a lot of traffic.

Remember, when it comes to social media, it's a never-ending flow of things, and yours will get pushed down quickly by new posts. You need to maximize your exposure and the number of people who see and interact with it by paying attention to what the ideal times are for your particular audience. For my local blog, I know that if I post links on my Facebook page on the weekend, it's largely ineffective. My reports show that my audience isn't online much on the weekend. Therefore, I post during the week when I know they are more likely to see it.

THE BEST PROMOTIONAL TOOL

Coming full circle, I have to reiterate the fact that I believe the most important thing you can do to promote your blog is to work on your blog. Create great content that people want and need. When you do that, the readers will not only come back to use your site time and again, but they will do the promoting for you. They will want others to know about your blog, so they will start sharing it with others. They will post and share particular articles on your site. Good blogs get people talking, which is promotion for you that doesn't take your time or bust your budget.

Quality content and giving people useful information is what will bring people to your site, bring them back to your site, and get them to bring their friends and family to your site. If the content is good, you won't have to do a lot of promoting of your blog because it will attract an audience that will come back to it and help promote it for you. I work weekdays, splitting my time each day between my writing work, such as writing books, ghostblogging, writing articles, and working on copywriting projects, and working on my blogs. While I may spend hours some days working on my blogs, I probably put a total of fifteen minutes per day into promoting them. The vast majority of my time is spent on the blogs themselves, with just a little time going to a few ways that I promote them. I could put more time into promoting them, but I'm not sure that it would be worth the trade-off in the time or money that would be spent or lost doing so. The system I have works for me, and I make a good salary from my blogs, so I am not going to fix what isn't broken, as the saying goes.

BLOGGER SPOTLIGHT
Kemi Ibeh
Musings and Adventures
www.musingsandadventures.com

When did you first start blogging and what got you interested in doing so?
I started in late January 2018. I've always wanted to do something creative, but didn't know what, as I'm not a photographer, MUA, or artist. I love to write and travel (when I can) so I researched this niche and added a sustainability slant to it as that is my passion as well.

What blogging format do you use, and are you happy with it?
WordPress. I don't code, so thankfully a non-coder like me can maneuver it.

How long did it take before you were making a good salary each year from your blog?
I have a full-time career so I don't rely on my blog for salary. We all know it takes a long while for a blog to replace your full-time salary and since I'm not a professional traveler to garner monthly press trips, this is still a side hustle. Still, within the first year, I've made up to $700 from writing gigs and complimentary product.

What did you find to be your biggest challenge in blogging, and how did you overcome it?
SEO and marketing! Prior to blogging, I had no idea what SEO was, or that so many things went behind the scenes to produce posts. I had to learn SEO on-the-go as well as writing in active tense, keywords, and all that. Let's not even start on daily social media engagement, lol. That is marketing on its own and you have to be comfortable with selling yourself and tooting your own horn; something I've never been used to.

What advice would you offer to new bloggers, or those who are still struggling to earn money from their blog?

Don't focus on money or you will lose your zeal and excitement that got you to begin blogging in the first place. Focus on putting out quality content and have a time frame, be it monthly or twice a month. Work on SEO and opportunities will come. All of my writing gigs came from media/content strategists who read my posts online and reached out to me to write on travel topics. Also, you could join influencer platforms or become an affiliate for favorite brands. Furthermore, some collaborations offer product or experiences in return (especially for lifestyle/fashion and travel), so not every compensation is in dollars.

What is one thing you have done that has helped you be able to earn more blogging?

Earn from some writing, affiliate and minimal complimentary products.

What is your top tip for bloggers who want to earn a salary from their blog?

Have emergency savings and a plan before you quit your job, because blogging is a crowded field and salary doesn't come fortnightly like a nine-to-five. Focus on putting out interesting and quality content as well. Good luck!

5

Monetizing Your Blog

Blogging can be a great way to make money. Blogging can be something you do on a part-time basis to have a side hustle, or it can be your full-time career. You can earn a great salary per year by blogging. The potential to make a living by blogging is there, and there are numerous ways to earn money from your blogs. It's all about finding which methods you like and which ones work for you.

I have numerous ways that I earn money from my blogs, and it all adds up to a nice yearly salary. One thing that is crucial that bloggers understand is that it takes patience. Rarely will you find a blogger who can start a blog and right away make decent money from it. Before you can start earning some money, you need to lay the foundation. By that, I mean that there is work to be done before you can start looking for ways to monetize your blog. You will need to make sure you have plenty of pages on your blog, that you have an audience, that you are getting traffic to the site, etc.

I have numerous blogs, but there are two of them that I started in 2009 just as something on the side. When I started them, I didn't expect to earn much money from them. I just liked the idea of the blogs and therefore I created them and put in a few hours per week to maintain them. I did this for two years, just laying the groundwork. After that point, I started thinking about how I could monetize my blogs to earn a little money from them each month. I went two years without ever earning a dime from them. That doesn't mean that you will put in two years of your time before you start earning. I hadn't even tried to make money from them during those first two years. I could have started making money from them much sooner, but the thought hadn't crossed my mind. I was making money from my freelance writing career, and the blogs were just something I was working on as a side project.

After the two years went by and I started to realize that I could earn money from the blogs, I dove in and started actively working toward monetizing them. It didn't take long before I was earning money from both of them. I also went on to offer my blog post writing services to others, which became lucrative as well. Many people think they can only make money from their own blogs, but if you are willing to blog for others, you can earn money that way, too.

BLOGGING PERKS

I like to refer to the non-money things you may receive as "blogging perks." As a blogger, you may end up receiving freebies. While they don't have monetary value, they can certainly add some fun to your life. You may be given things like free tickets to events or free products. Usually the company is doing that in exchange for you giving them a plug on your blog or social media page, or they would like you to do a formal review.

Once your blog is getting traffic, you will likely get offers each week or month for you to do some kind of review for a product or service. You can be selective in the ones you want to do. They can be time-consuming, so only agree to the ones that you feel are worth the time for you to do. If you do take a product and review it on your blog, you need to disclose to the reader that the item was given to you. We will delve more into disclosures in chapter 7, when we look at keeping your blog legal. But do keep in mind that you need to have a disclosure on your site that lets readers know you are receiving a product in exchange for a review. Having said that, I always still give an honest review, because that's my reputation as a blogger. If I give a great review to a poor product, then people will come to not trust me a as blogger. I have received products to try and I've not liked them at all. In those cases, I tend to not do the review and I kindly let the company know why. If I don't like a product, I don't want to hurt the company by putting out an unfavorable review, telling people to not waste their time purchasing it.

The blogging perks can be a fun and interesting addition to what you receive from your efforts. One week you may get complimentary tickets to a show, another you may get chocolate bars, and another you may receive some ice skating passes. If you have a family, these things can add up to provide some fun for the kids, without you having to put out extra money. I've known bloggers who get such perks as furniture, vacations, restaurant gift cards, and more.

Most of the salary that I earn each year from my blogs comes from a combination of display advertising and advertising networks. I do earn money through other routes, such as affiliate links, but that's where most of the money is generated that is directly related to my blogs. Being a freelance writer, I also make money each year by blogging for numerous other individuals and companies. I don't sell those services on my blogs, though; they are services offered through my freelance writing site.

WAYS TO MONETIZE YOUR BLOG

This is in no way an exhaustive list of ways that you can earn money from your blog. There are bloggers who get creative and are able to find additional ways to earn money and perks from their blog. Consider the following ways, and maybe even try some out, to see what works for you and which ones your target market responds to.

Display Advertising

This is when you will have advertisers contact you directly to pay to have their ad displayed on your site. The ads will typically link to their website, and you can have them show up a certain number of times per month, or they can show up on every page view. It's just a matter of what you arrange. Some advertisers like the idea of you using ad-serving software, so you can provide them with a report that shows each month how many times their ad was shown and how many times it was clicked on.

Using this advertising tracking software for the ads on the website was part of my job when I was working at Vegas.com, and I went to San Francisco for training to use the program. While I understand how the programs work and could implement one on my blogs, I don't. This is because there is an expense that comes with using such software and I haven't invested in it. Plus, I've only had two or three people over the last ten years ask me about such software, so I don't feel that there are enough of my advertisers who want it to warrant me investing in it. If you sell display advertising, you can sell it based on your own terms.

I always advise my advertisers that they should track where their traffic comes from. That way they know if their marketing efforts and dollars are paying off. They can look at their own analytics to see where their traffic is coming from, and they can ask their customers how they heard of them. If they are doing this, they will know if the money they are spending advertising on your site is worth the return on investment.

Some people may want to pay a rate based on a CPM, which is cost per thousand impressions. Another option is to charge a flat rate per week, month, or year, or whatever works for you. I sell a lot of display advertising on my blogs and I usually sell it for six- to twelve-month increments. I do this because that way I lock an advertiser in, rather than looking for a new one to fill the space every month. I have the person pay for the whole campaign up front, and then I contact them a few weeks before it expires to see if they would like to renew. I also take short-term display advertising, such as to promote a particular event or promotion. Those may last a week or month at the most. Display advertising works really well if you have a localized blog where you can get local companies to want to advertise on your site.

Advertising Networks

There are numerous advertising networks that you can sign up with to earn money from. Google Ads is a popular one that people use. They get all the advertisers, and you just put the code onto your page. They will serve up the ads, and you earn money from how much they are shown, as well as when people click on them. Advertising networks can be a simple way to earn money on your blogs, provided you get decent traffic to it. I use Google Ads and personally know other bloggers who use it as well. You have to pay attention to which ads tend to work the best, so you can capitalize on using that particular kind more, which will increase your revenue.

While many bloggers use Google Ads, there are a lot of other networks that offer the same type of service. You can check out the different ones to determine which one you think makes a good fit for your site. I've been satisfied with my experience with Google Ads, so I have stuck with them for years, despite other ad networks approaching me about switching to theirs. When you hook up with an advertising network, you will create ads that will fit on your pages, where you would like them to show up. The network provides you with a code, which you put on your blog so that the ad shows up in that space. The code also tracks all the advertising information, and you should be able to log into your advertising network account to review reports that show how many times it showed ads on your site, how much you made, and which ads are making you the most money.

Influencer Posts

If your blog or social media page has a lot of followers, you may be approached for what are referred to as "influencer posts." When you have a large following, you are considered to be someone who can influence your followers, and this appeals to companies that also want to reach your audience. Rather than engaging in display advertising, where they are touting their products, the companies will work with those who are considered influencers in order to get their product or service information out there. While the logistics of what all is involved may vary, they may hire you to post pictures of their products, do a write-up on them, make a video, have a giveaway of their products, etc.

There are many ways they can work with you to reach your audience, and you will be paid for that exposure you are giving them. There are some celebrities who get paid a lot of money for influencer posts. It's been reported that Kylie Jenner gets $1 million per paid Instagram post, Selena Gomez gets $800,000 per influencer post, and soccer star Cristiano Ronaldo gets $750,000 per influencer post. If you follow these people on their social media pages, you can usually spot which posts are the paid influencer ones.

They are typically promoting a particular product, such as a watch, fragrance, or other item. While celebrities make an incredible amount of money for their influencer posts, bloggers who have a large following can still make money by doing this, even if it's on a smaller scale. Each of these influencer posts helps add up to a good annual salary from your blogging efforts.

Presentations

As a blogger, you are establishing yourself as an expert in something, which is the topic you are blogging about. As such, you may be able to earn money from being paid to give presentations on those topics. To find paid presentation opportunities, you will want to list that as a service on your blog, but also look for events and conferences that are taking place that relate to your subject matter. Conferences, for example, are often looking for people to give presentations, and they will pay for the service. You can also arrange your own presentations and get paid to do them by getting paid sponsorships for them or by having the attendees purchase tickets to the event. Giving presentations may also open the door to you being able to promote and sell additional products that you may have on the topic.

Selling Products

Many bloggers have something they can personally sell, which helps them earn a living from their efforts. Whether it is books, courses, or something you have created, you can make money from selling a product on your blog. Blogs can be a great marketing tool to bring in your target market, and then you will have items to offer them that they can purchase. Likewise, you may get your product ideas from your blog. If you have a blog that has become popular, you may be able to create products that are related to it and the theme and then sell those items.

Whether it is offering your readers T-shirts, tote bags, ebooks, or book-marks, there are many options that you can consider in order to generate an income. Think about what it is that your target market would want to pur-chase, and then go from there, if you have the blog and want to add products to sell. If you already have products you want to sell, then create the blog and reach your target market by producing content that relates to what you are selling. The options for this are as diverse as the blog topics that are out there.

Sell Courses

Some bloggers have a skill set that they can sell to others. Perhaps you teach how to decorate cakes, make aquafaba, or have a workout program like no other. You could create an online course and then use your blog to bring in your target market and sell it to them. There are some very popular bloggers who earn their money from this method. One of my favorite blogs, Zen Habits, which is run by Leo Babauta, has no advertisers on the blog. The blogger earns his money from driving traffic to the blog, and then selling courses and books that relate to the content on his blog. His blog is not filled with attempts to sell you anything either, but if you sign up for his emails, which millions of people have, he subtly plugs those courses into the posts that he sends out.

Offer Services

Most bloggers have skills that they can offer to others for a fee. These include coaching services, writing, graphic arts, or blog creation. There are compa-nies and individuals who will pay for these services. As I've mentioned in a previous chapter, there are businesses and individuals that would like to have a blog, but they may not want to put in the time and effort to have one. They will then hire a freelancer to do the work for them. You should mention somewhere on your blog that you offer these services. Whether you are hired to create their blog or write posts for it ongoing, you will need to determine what you are comfortable making for these services. In addition to having people come to you to inquire about these freelance services you offer, you can also go to online job sites where you bid on projects, such as Guru.com.

There are many people who post jobs that they need done on those sites, and then freelancers will submit a bid to say how much they charge for the project. The employer would then select someone to do the work. Many people seek out coaches in their respective fields. If you offer coaching services, you can have a revenue stream by helping others to become successful or figure out what it is that they want or need to do. Coaching services are a popular way for people to make money, and they can be offered online, through email, by phone, video calls, and in person. You have a lot of options when it comes to how you will handle coaching services, so you can offer it to people locally and from afar.

Sponsorships

While it's not display advertising, it's close to it. You can seek companies to become sponsors of your blog, and pay a fee for doing so. Whether you have one main sponsor or half a dozen, it can add up and contribute to your annual blogging salary. It's helpful to seek out sponsors that would make a good fit for the type of blog you have. For example, if you have a blog about children, seek out sponsorships from hospitals, companies that make baby products, or those that offer services for families. For every type of blog or topic, there is a sponsor that would make a good fit. The arrangements you make with the sponsor can vary, including offering display advertising, influencer posts, being called the site sponsor, and more.

Affiliate Programs

There are bloggers who make the bulk of their salary from affiliate programs. These are programs that pay you a commission for sending the company traffic or getting people to buy things. You can check out many affiliate programs by joining a site like Commission Junction. One of the most popular commission programs used by bloggers is the one offered by Amazon. You sign up for these affiliate programs and once approved you can create posts where you link particular products or pages, sending traffic to those items. If people purchase, you will end up earning a commission from their purchase. Whether you purposely create posts to promote specific products, or you simply affiliate link products you already planned to write about, you can earn money by using affiliate links on your site. In addition to adding the links to your posts, you can create ads on your site that will link to particular affiliate products or pages.

Webinars

Similar to getting paid to do presentations, offering webinars is another way you can earn money from your blog. You can use the blog as your platform to bring in an audience and promote your webinars, which people pay to attend. Webinars are offered online, so you can have this type of revenue stream without ever leaving your home office. You can offer webinars on a variety of things that cover your blog's subject matter. There are online services that host the webinars.

Event Hosting

No matter what type of blog you have, you can host events. Consider the type of blog you have, what the themes are, and then determine what type of event makes sense for you do. When one of my blogs turned five years old, I held a community event, where many businesses paid to have a table set up. I also had companies that paid to sponsor the event. The event gave the people in the community a fun place to take their kids to, and it added to my blogging revenue for that year. You can have events on a monthly, quarterly, or yearly basis. Determine what works for you, and you may find that it is a lucrative opportunity for you to engage in.

Creating Content

While you know at this point that you can create content for your blog and do it for other people's, you can also focus on creating blogs simply as a place to add content. If you create blogs that offer a lot of useful information, they may get a good amount of traffic each month, and you can use things like affiliate links and advertising networks to generate a monthly income from them. You want to focus on quality content, of course, but if you can produce a lot of it, then you can create a site that gets good traffic.

Aim for blog post articles that are evergreen, so that the information will remain relevant for a long time. Imagine if you wrote one blog post every morning for a year to put on the blog. After a year, you would have hundreds of articles that have affiliate links and ads that are generating an income. The posts shouldn't take you long, maybe an hour each day, so you can still fit in doing all of your other work as well. Once this is set up, it is passive income. You can let it just keep getting traffic and do minimal work to keep it up.

PATIENCE BEFORE APPROACHING

When you start your blog, you may be in a hurry to start making money from it. But as I've already shared, it can take some time. You have to be patient and allow your blog to grow and for you to gain an audience. Some of the revenue streams listed above require that you have an established presence before being associated with it. In order to approach people regarding display advertising, sponsorships, or other such avenues, you have to have a well-established blog that has a following. If you want to earn money from advertising networks, you will need to get a good and steady amount of traffic to your blog. Advertising networks rely upon your having traffic to your site.

It's important to keep in mind that when you are quoting someone a price for something, you don't use an hourly rate. While you may have an hourly rate in your head, it could shock the person that you are giving the quote to. Rather than tell them that you want to make fifty dollars per hour writing blog posts for their corporate blog, you should say that you will be charging them a flat fee of seventy-five dollars per blog post of a certain length. You should do the math and calculations and let them know the flat rate. If you tell someone you want fifty dollars per hour, or whatever the number may be, they may immediately turn away. It could be more than they make, or it may seem like a really high number to them. It's okay for you to know what it equals out to per hour, but keep that information to yourself and just quote people using a flat rate.

Whether for advertising sales or for your services, people may want to negotiate the rate. There's nothing wrong with doing this, as long as you are comfortable with it. There's no hard and fast rules about how to negotiate, so go with what you are comfortable with. As long as you are comfortable with the rate you are getting for the exposure they are getting, or the services you are providing, then everything is fine. People like to feel as though they got a deal or that they negotiated a better deal, so there's nothing wrong with giving someone a discount or meeting them at a rate that everyone is comfortable with.

When you approach people regarding advertising or teaming up with your blog, or if they approach you, will need to be able to answer some questions about your blog. Some of the things they will want to know include your blog's analytics. The information on tracking your blog will be covered in-depth in chapter 6, but you will want to be prepared to answer questions regarding how much traffic your blog gets, how many visitors it has, etc. They may even want to know what the demographics of your traffic are, such as if they are male, female, or what country or area of the world they are from. There is no need to stress over being able to answer such questions. You will have the tools you need to answer these questions and more.

We'd all love to start earning money from blogging as soon as we throw our first post out there, but that's just not the reality of it. With working at it, being persistent, and staying focused, you will grow the blog, the audience, traffic, and a revenue stream. There is a lot of money to be made in blogging, if you have patience, persistence, and perseverance.

BLOGGER SPOTLIGHT

Diane Bedard

Nature Coaster

www.naturecoaster.com

When did you first start blogging and what got you interested in doing so?

In 2014. I used to publish a printed publication for visitors about Florida's Nature Coast. It went belly-up in 2010 due to print and distribution costs. I was recovering from major trauma and had to sit in a chair to heal and began wondering what I would do with the rest of my life. The thought came, "What if I took the magazine online?"

What blogging format do you use, and are you happy with it?

I use WordPress. I am quite happy with it. Self-taught and then I hired a web design and marketing firm to manage it.

How long did it take before you were making a good salary each year from your blog?

Four years.

What did you find to be your biggest challenge in blogging, and how did you overcome it?

First, I was blessed with an amazing mentor, Robin Draper of Authentic Florida. She encouraged me and believed in me when I was losing faith. It really helped stick and stay to win.

Hiring someone to manage the technical side so I could be freed up to create and sell. I am a good writer—award-winning—and a good salesperson, so I needed to hire people to fill in the gaps so I could bring the publication into profitability.

Also, I need help in managing the calendar/editorial schedule. That will be the next area of delegation and growth.

What advice would you offer to new bloggers, or those who are still struggling to earn money from their blog?

I had to give up my freelance gigs and concentrate solely on my blog. It required my full attention, or I needed to give it up. I also needed to really promote NatureCoaster.com with a professional media kit—with real numbers from Google Analytics. Demographics are imperative in selling advertising.

What is one thing you have done that has helped you be able to earn more blogging?

Selling advertising directly to advertisers.

What is your top tip for bloggers who want to earn a salary from their blog?

First, you MUST publish regularly. Second, create an email list. Third, join organizations that promote what you do and enter your work in their award contest. Having an award-winning blog sets you above a lot of competition.

Analyze your blog's Google Analytics. Where is your market? Who is your blog's market? Then look for partners who want to reach that market. Create a professional media kit and ask for the sale. If they say no, ask why. Use that information to help you improve.

6

Tracking Your Blog's Success

Once you get your blog going, you can't simply walk away and go do something else. Well, you can for a while, but at some point you are going to want to know how well it's doing. You will want to know if it's not doing well at all, too, so that you can take measures to make changes and bring more traffic to it. It's a good idea to track your blog's success so you can get a feeling for how many people are visiting your blog, how many page views you are getting, and additional pertinent information.

Tracking your blog is not difficult, but you will need to know some of the tools of the trade in order to be able to do so. There are a lot of different kinds of plug-ins and companies that offer tracking information. Some are free, while others you will need to pay for. I've tried paying for some and found that I get no more information than I get for free from other services. Therefore, I tend to skip paying for any type of tracking and stick with using the free information. It hasn't failed me yet, so I'll keep using it until and if it ever does.

YOUR FIRST STEPS TOWARD TRACKING

Once your blog is up and running, you want to let the search engines know that you exist. After a while they would figure it out anyway, but it's a good idea to move it along faster by submitting your URL into search engines to let them know that you have a site up and you would like it included in their search engine. Over a decade ago there were numerous popular search engines that were used, and people would go to each one and submit their website URL with each one of them. Today, there are only a handful of search engines that are popular, so at the very least, you want to get your website URL submitted into Google.

Love Google or hate Google (I tend to love Google), they rule the world. It's estimated that they have 90 percent of the search engine market in the world. It's also estimated that every second, they receive around 63,000 searches, with the average person doing three to four Google searches per day. It's incredible how much Google is used. And as such, your blog needs to be in there. You want Google serving up your information as often as possible and as close to the first page as possible. Most people who do searches don't go far beyond the first one or two pages of search results.

Having said all that, the first place you want to submit your URL to would be Google. Go to Google and type in "submit URL to Google." From there they will provide you with the instructions on how to submit your URL to them. When you register your site with them, you will have a Search Console. This console will be beneficial in helping you see what information they have on your URL once it's been submitted and indexed, and it will provide you with detailed information on how your blog is performing.

Once you submit your URL to Google and other search engines, don't expect it to show up immediately. It usually takes a little time before it shows up. Once it is in there, you also can't expect it to show up on the first page of results for searches that are not your blog's specific name. Whatever it is that you are blogging about, it will take time before it starts working its way higher into the search results. You will get higher results by producing good content that is relevant to what is being searched for, and if people like your site. If your blog is optimized, meaning you have used good keywords that will help the search engines be able to find it when relevant searches are done, you will have a better chance at being found and put into search results. Google uses what are called crawlers to find your site and read the information that is on it. The crawlers are automated. They review your website pages and index specific information that is on the pages so that it is ready to be served up once someone does a relevant search.

You can also help your website show up higher in search results by having other sites link to yours. This is the important role that backlinks play. If a lot of sites are linking to yours, then Google's tool assumes that your site must be pretty credible and be providing trustworthy information. Remember, in order for Google to be the best search engine in the world, it's in their best interest to ensure that they are providing people with good results when they do searches.

Another issue that will help is to make sure you are naming your images something that is relevant to what you have posted. If your image name is

"1mg001," then Google has no idea what that picture is of. But if you are posting a recipe of a homemade vegan apple pie and you label the image "vegan_apple_pie," it will help in the search results. You can also use an alt text "Vegan Apple Pie Recipe" that will also help.

USING GOOGLE ANALYTICS

Once your blog is in the search engines, you will also want a way to track it through analytics. I use Google Analytics, but as I mentioned earlier, there are other sources you can use. It's not a bad idea once you get going to try a few of the paid options to see if you get additional information that you are pleased with, so you can see if it's worth paying for it. I feel I get enough from Google Analytics, but others may feel that they need more, so it's a matter of what works for you and what your goals are.

Google will monitor the traffic to your site through their Analytics tool. Then you will be able to log in at any time and get detailed information about your blog. You can create the account with them and then let them know which of your websites you want them to monitor the traffic on. They will provide you with a code that you need to put onto your blog in order for them to be able to gather the traffic information. Once you place the piece of code onto your blog, following their directions, they will quietly gather information in the background. There's nothing else you will need to do in order for them to obtain the details.

At any time, you will be able to log into your Google Analytics account and see what's going on with your site. Once you log in, you will be able to see how many people are active on your blog at that moment, what they are looking at, where your traffic is coming from, how well you retain users, what country your users live in, and what type of device they are using to access your site. The Analytics tool provides a lot of detailed information. You can play around with it to look at the details for the last week, month, or even a year.

Using Google Analytics is free, and it can give you a wealth of information about the traffic to your blog. Google Analytics will give you an excellent snapshot of what is going on with your blog. You will be able to see the most viewed pages, where your traffic is coming from, and even the most popular times that people visit your site. Some of these things may be of interest to you, and others you may not feel you have a need for. The good thing is you can pick and choose what is meaningful for you and what you can use to further grow your site.

For example, if you look at the pages that your visitors view, you can see what's popular on your site. If there are standout topics that are much more popular than others, you may want to focus on writing more posts on those topics. You may also want to go back to those popular pages and add in some more advertising or affiliate links (where it makes sense to do so). You can also use this information to sell sponsorships on those pages to display advertisers.

You can also look at the acquisition information to see where your traffic is coming from. This will let you know if your social media promotion efforts are paying off or how many people type your address in directly. You will also see how much "organic search" traffic you are getting, which is how many people are coming to your site from search engines. You want that number to be high, because that means you have done a good job with the SEO on your site. In other words, you have made your content easy for the search engines to find and serve it up in results.

Another acquisition source it will show you is how many people came to your site through referrals. If you click on that, you will get detailed information regarding what other sites have linked to your site. This can be interesting to take a look at, because it shows what type of sites are posting or choosing to link to your site.

Google offers an Analytics Academy, where you can take free online courses to learn more about how to understand and use your analytic information. They offer a free class for beginners, advanced, power users, and more. Taking one or more of those courses will help you become more comfortable with understanding analytics.

OTHER GOOGLE TOOLS

Google provides other tools that you can use as well. You can use their tool to conduct a mobile-friendly test and to evaluate your website's page speed. When you view your analytics, you will be able to see what percentage of your viewers go to your blog on a desktop computer, their tablet, or their phone. You may be surprised at how many people use their phone today to access your site. If that is the case, you want your blog to be mobile-friendly.

Google offers a "mobile-friendly test" that you can use for free. Simply google the page for it and then when on the page, add your blog's URL into the box on the page. Click on "test URL" and they will run a fast test to see if your site is mobile-friendly. In today's world, with everyone using phones, your blog has to be mobile-friendly so that you don't lose out on traffic. Within a minute Google will let you know if they think your website is mobile-friendly or not. If it is, great, then there's nothing you need to do. If they say it's not, then you need to take action to make it mobile-friendly. Using a responsive website design will help to ensure that your blog is mobile-friendly.

Have you ever gone to a website that was simply taking too much time to load and so you gave up? I know I have, and there's probably a good chance you have as well. There can be times that it's a short-lived issue that is resolved when you hit the reload button. But there are times when people may have a really slow website. When that is the case, they will lose some traffic. There will always be some people who don't want to wait for the site to come up and will close out and move on.

You can check the speed of your website using a Google tool called PageSpeed Insights. Once you google that and bring up the page, enter your blog's URL into the tool and click on the analyze button. Within a minute or two, they will provide you a report that rates your blog's loading speed. They will also give you tips on ways that you can improve it. You can read those things to see if there are actions you want to take in order to improve your site's loading time.

ALEXA RANKING

Websites that get traffic will have what is called an Alexa Ranking. You can monitor your Alexa Ranking to see how popular your blog is (or isn't). To get the information, log on to Alexa.com and scroll down the page to where it says "Browse Top Sites." Enter your blog's URL in that box and click "find." If your blog doesn't get much traffic at all, you likely won't see a ranking. It will instead say that there's not enough information available.

If your blog does get enough traffic to rank, Alexa will give you a ranking number. The global ranking number is where your blog ranks among all the sites in the world in terms of traffic. Keep in mind that the lower the number, the better. Keep in mind that one estimate puts the number of websites in the world at over 1.5 billion as of the time of writing this. Therefore, if your blog ranks 1.5 million, it's not too bad and it means you are getting some steady traffic to the site. The website ranked number one in the world? You guessed it, Google!

The snapshot of information that Alexa provides can be useful when it comes to monitoring the growth of your blog. They will give you information about what keywords people are using to find your site, how many sites are linking into your blog, similar sites, and more. They will also provide you with some SEO keyword information that you can use when it comes to writing new posts. They offer a paid option, where they will give you more detailed information about keyword opportunities for your specific site.

If you choose to have a paid subscription, you can use the information to help grow your traffic. They will give you keyword opportunities, and if they make sense to you for the focus of your blog, you can incorporate them. You may want to write posts specifically around those keywords, since they are an opportunity to bring in more traffic to your site.

When reviewing Alexa keyword rankings, keep in mind that the lower score is better. Those with lower scores are getting more traffic to their blog. It's also important to note that if a site is part of a national site, it will skew the results, so you will not get an accurate picture of the website's traffic. For example, if there is a main company that allows franchises in cities around the country, but each URL is based off that main one, you will get an Alexa Ranking for the site as a whole. You won't get a ranking for that individual franchise. The traffic rating will be inflated, making it get a better ranking, simply because it is pulling traffic from around the country. That doesn't mean it pertains to your specific franchise and the traffic it gets just in your area. You will get more accurate results when blogs are on their own URL and not an extension of a parent company.

UNDERSTANDING YOUR ANALYTICS

When you are reviewing the analytics for your blog, you may wonder what everything means. You can gather a wealth of information about your blog, but if you don't know what the terms mean, then it won't do you much good. Here are some of the terms you will see when reviewing your analytics and what they mean.

Page views. A page view is tracked every time someone looks at a full page on your blog. The number of page views shows how many pages were viewed in any given time frame. Of course, you want a lot of page views, because it means that people are looking at a lot of content on your site.

Entry page. This is the first page that someone saw when they came to your blog. Many people will not come in on your main page, because they will have found subsequent pages in search engines or have been led there from links.

Exit page. This is the last page that the person was looking at before they left your blog. If you notice a pattern of people leaving on a particular page, you may want to take a look at it to see if you can change it up a bit so that you are not losing so many people on that one page. Perhaps offering a link to another page that may interest them will do the trick.

Paid referrals. You will only see numbers here if you are paying for your site to be promoted, such as through Google AdSense. If you don't have any advertising campaigns going on, then you should expect no activity here. If you are paying for advertising, you want to pay attention to this, so you can determine if the advertising is worth the return on investment. Consider how much you are spending on advertising and how many people it is bringing to your site, so you can see how much it's costing you per person.

Direct referrals. These are the people who typed your URL into the address bar to go right to your blog, or they had it bookmarked and clicked on it. This is in comparison to the number of people who come to your site through searches and referrals. When your blog name is new, you shouldn't expect much here, but once your blog name has been established, you will see this number increase. When you have loyal fans who go back to your site regularly, they will type in the name, increasing this figure.

Organic search. This is the number of people who found their way to your blog by doing searches. They are not from any kind of advertising or paid searches; they just typed something into the search engine that ultimately led them to your site.

Bounce rate. This number shows you how many people come to your site to look at one page and then leave it to go to another website or close out altogether. They only view one page on your blog and then are done. If you can get people to click to another page and then another, you will have a lower bounce rate. Of course, you want to keep people on your blog, looking at many pages, if at all possible. However, that is not always possible. There are some things, such as a post about event information, where that may be the only thing of interest to the users. Your bounce rate is really going to be influenced by the content your blog has, as well as the effort you put into trying to keep people looking at subsequent pages. It's considered average if you have a bounce rate of up to 40 percent.

Session duration. This is the average amount of time that a user spends on your website. Again, you want them to spend as much time as possible, but that's not always going to be possible. A lot has to do with the type of blog you have and content they are looking at, as well as the effort you put in to keep them there longer.

Users. This is the total number of people who visited your blog during any given time period. A "unique visitor total" is the number of different people who visited the site at least once during the time period.

Pages per session. This shows you the average number of pages that people are viewing once they come to your blog. You should also see your average session time, which gives you the average amount of time that a person spends on your website.

The amount of information you can get from reviewing your analytics is eye-opening. You will be able to learn a lot about who your readers are. You can gain such information about your blog visitors as demographics, age, gender, interests, languages, how you acquired them, and more. Logging into Google Analytics alone, you will have a wealth of information at your fingertips about your blog.

WHY ANALYTICS MATTER

By now you have been inundated with a little of the technical side of blogging. I get that it may not seem quite so interesting from the start. There are a lot of numbers and a lot of information, but you may wonder what you even need all of this for. Or if you even need it at all. Well, there are numerous reasons why this information is good to have, to access, and to pay attention to.

One of the main reasons that you will want to know and understand the analytics side of blogging is because you want to make money from your efforts. When you know more about how to understand your analytics, you can use that information to increase your blogging revenue.

If you want to sell direct advertising to companies, such as in the form of display ads, you will need to know some of these things. In order to even begin offering advertising to companies, you need to know about your blog. You need to be able to tell potential advertisers how many page views your blog gets each year, how many users visit your site each month, who is it that visits your blog, and so on.

For my local parenting blog, I use this information to sell advertising to companies that want to reach my audience. I have gathered the information from my analytics that shows that on average, there are 23,000 people per month that visit that site. Some months there are double and triple that, depending on what is going on in the area. After all, it's a blog that focuses just on providing event information for parents in my county. I typically sell advertising based on a yearlong contract. I also know from my analytics that there has been over 1.1 million page views in the last year, that 80 percent of the traffic to the site is female, and I have even narrowed down the most popular age ranges.

No matter what information it is that my potential advertisers are looking for, I can take a look at my analytics and likely provide them with an answer. On their end, they use my analytics to determine if it's worth spending the money to advertise on my site. If I tell them that it's going to be $1,200 to have an ad on the site for a year, they want to do a little math on their own to see if it makes sense for them to go forward with the campaign. Any blogger who wants to sell direct advertising on their blog needs to get comfortable with analytic information.

If you are earning money from advertising networks, such as Google AdSense, you can use your analytics to increase your earnings as well. Analytics will show you the most popular pages on your site, which are the ones that people are viewing the most. You can use that information to add some more ad code to the page. You can also add in affiliate links to those pages to increase earnings. By seeing your most popular pages, you can also find sponsors for those pages. For example, let's say that one of your most popular pages is all about quinoa. You could seek a quinoa producer to sponsor the page, or anyone else who would be interested in sponsoring that page for a fee. If you try and can't find a sponsor to pay for the position, you can always add an affiliate link to sell a related product.

Finally, you can use your analytics information to grow your blog, which in turn will also increase your earnings. Reviewing all the detailed information about your blog lets you learn more about what your audience likes to look at, where your traffic is coming from, what your popular enter pages are, and so on. All of these details give you information that you can use to help increase how long people are on your site, decide what to blog about, etc.

The more you get comfortable with your blog analytics, the more you will get to know who your readers are, what they like to read, how to improve your SEO, and more. All of this is important to your blog's success and to earning money from your efforts. You will be able to see what works and what doesn't, among many other valuable pieces of information. Don't worry if when you first start reviewing the analytics, it all seems so strange. There's a learning curve, but you will get it all, you will be able to understand it, and you will be able to use it grow your blog and income.

When you first start your blog, don't expect a lot in terms of analytics. It takes patience. You need to grow your blog and focus on putting a lot of good content on there. Find ways to keep people on the site longer, by having links in your blog posts that link to other blog posts of yours. You want to find ways to get your readers to engage and be interested in what your blog offers. The more you do that, the traffic will come, and so too will the earnings.

Everyone wants their blog to be popular when they hit the publish button. But that's just not the reality of it. It takes effort, focus, and patience to grow your blog and earn money from it. Many people give up and walk away from the blog because they go into it thinking that blogging will make them rich within months. Blogging is not a get-rich scheme. Not at all. Yes, you can earn a good living from blogging, but it won't happen overnight. You have to be committed, learn the tools of the trade, and keep working at it. I've had blogs for many years, and even today I still feel they are a work in progress. I'm always looking for ways to improve them, grow them, and earn more from them.

BLOGGER SPOTLIGHT
Chandra Waters
A Gullah Girl
www.agullahgirl.com

When did you first start blogging and what got you interested in doing so?

I have been blogging off and on since 2014. I majored in English—mainly because I loved writing. Unfortunately, my career path did not lead to the opportunity to do a lot of creative writing. I needed an outlet to get some of my creative musings out, and began blogging to do so.

What blogging format do you use, and are you happy with it?

I blog from WordPress. It does meet the requirements for my current blog, but I want to expand my content a bit so I am exploring other methods of getting my content out via social media outlets and email marketing.

How long did it take before you were making a good salary each year from your blog?

At this time I work full-time and blogging is my side hustle and one of my creative outlets. I'm currently at a level where I receive compensation for product testing and exclusive event invitations. It has not replaced my current salary.

What did you find to be your biggest challenge in blogging, and how did you overcome it?

My biggest challenge is consistency. I am learning to overcome this by automation and planning content. There are many free online content calendars out there for days when the blog ideas are few and far between. Also, repurposing evergreen content is a great way to keep your blog active.

What advice would you offer to new bloggers, or those who are still struggling to earn money from their blog?

Find your tribe. Write content that piques the interest of your followers. Tweak your SEOs and make sure that you use tags and keywords that your followers use in their everyday search for your content—not overly technical. Take the opportunity to use affiliate links when possible. Collaborate for exposure to other audiences.

What is one thing you have done that has helped you be able to earn more blogging?

Networking has led to many opportunities.

What is your top tip for bloggers who want to earn a salary from their blog?

There is power in community. Connect to someone who is doing what you want to do and seek them out as a mentor. In doing this, be respectful and remember time is money—so don't expect that all mentorship will be free. Be willing to pay or barter for the expertise (but make sure you're getting advice from an expert and not a novice).

7

Keeping It Legal

The last thing that most bloggers want to hear about are legal issues. Trust me when I say I get it. But trust me again when I say that as boring as legal issues may be, they are important to be aware of. Legal issues are never fun to hear about, but knowing about them can save you a lot of headache and time later on, should you do something that is considered illegal.

It seems as though you should be able to simply put your blog up, earn money, and never have to worry about legal issues. That would be nice if that were the case, but it's just not how it works. There are things that we bloggers have to know about and adhere to so we don't get ourselves into trouble. It's better to learn about these things now, rather than learning about them as you try to defend yourself from something later on. This chapter will focus on some of the most common legal issues that every blogger should keep in mind.

LEGAL NAMES

If you are going to use your name for your blog and when getting paid, then you won't need to do anything regarding filing a fictitious name. However, if your blog name has nothing do with your legal name and you will be collecting money under the blog name, rather than your own name, then you will need to file a fictitious name. In some states, this is called a DBA (doing business as). It simply lets the state know that you are legally collecting money under a name that is not your own.

I regularly receive payments that are made out to my blog name, Volusia County Moms. As such, I maintain having a fictitious name registered with the state. That way it is publicly known that Jacqueline Bodnar is doing business as Volusia County Moms and being paid in that name. It's usually an afford-able route to take, costing around fifty dollars for a five-year registration.

If people are making out payments to your blog name, rather than your personal name, you will also likely need to go to your bank and make a change to your account name. For example, in order for me to be able to deposit checks made out to Volusia County Moms, that name has to be on my bank account. My bank account has both my legal name and my fictitious name, so that checks can be deposited into the account that are made out to either name.

Some bloggers opt to take it a step further and create a legal business, such as a limited liability company (LLC). This is an option you can take. It does cost more to file and maintain an LLC. You may want to speak with an accountant if you have questions about how it could impact your yearly tax situation.

By the way, when it comes to the name of your blog, you also need to keep it legal. Avoid using someone else's company name, which could get you into trouble. You don't want to spend time growing your blog only to have a company come along and claim trademark infringement. It's not a good idea to use a company or product name in your blog name if it's not your own company or product.

GETTING PAID

As bloggers, we want to make money. That's what this book is about, after all. You want to put your blogging skills to work earning an income. But with that comes legal issues. Many people may wonder how you go about getting paid for starters. This is a common question that people have. There is no one set way you have to be paid for your blogging, and some income sources may dictate how you get paid, without you having many options.

If you are getting paid from advertising networks, for example, you will likely end up with a direct deposit type of situation. I have been get-ting money deposited directly into my bank account every month for years from Google. Once per month, they pay you for the prior month's earnings, with the funds seamlessly going right into your bank account. If you have an affiliate account with a place like Amazon, you can opt to get paid via check (which they charge a fee for), or you can take the funds each month in an Amazon gift card. If you are selling display advertising on your site to indi-vidual companies, you can let them know how you prefer to be paid.

To get paid from individual companies, you can request a check, bank deposit, or payment through PayPal. I've been paid through all three routes from my advertisers. I mostly opt to get paid through PayPal. They do take a cut for using the service, but I like the immediate nature of it. If you don't mind waiting for a check to be sent in the mail, you can avoid paying those fees and keep more money in your pocket. While the most common way I get paid is by PayPal, I do also have some clients who pay by check. If I have a client who prefers to pay by check, I'm completely fine with that as well.

When it comes to using PayPal, they have a tool in there that you can use to create invoices that get sent directly to people. You just send it to the advertiser's email address and use their invoice to detail what the transaction is about. Another nice thing about using PayPal for some payments is that they have a tool where you can create buttons or graphics for your site. If you are selling something specific, for example, you can create a button that allows readers to click on it and be taken directly to PayPal to make the payment. You can sell things like books, ebooks, subscriptions, and advertising using this.

I have an advertising marketplace on my blog, which is like a local business directory. It has local companies in it that my audience would be interested in. I have it set up so that businesses can join the marketplace at any time of the day or night. There is a page detailing the information about what they get by being in the marketplace, and they can also pay right there. All they have to do is click on the button, make the payment through PayPal, and then they will be taken to a page that thanks them for joining. Meanwhile, anytime someone joins, I get a message from PayPal that money has been received. I can then take a look at it to read that someone joined the marketplace. It's a seamless process, and it creates a revenue stream that is always available without me having to constantly have a hand on it.

TAXES TALK

It should only make sense that we follow up discussing getting paid by talking about taxes. If you are going to earn money from blogging, you are going to have to pay taxes on those earnings. That's the law, and there's no way around it. While the threshold can change, at this time, if you are under sixty-five years old and gross under $12,000 for the year, you won't have to file. But if you plan to make more than that, which you should and will if you are committed to it, then you will need to file a tax return.

Anytime you receive payments, you need to keep track of how much you are earning. You can use an accounting software program, such as QuickBooks, a spreadsheet, or you can keep records by hand in a notebook. How you keep the records is your call and not nearly as important as the fact that you do keep track of any income that is coming in.

At the end of the year, you will need to take a look at what you grossed and then determine if you need to file taxes on it. You may want to speak with an accountant for clarification so that you remain legal. If you are working a job and earning money from blogging, it's possible that you will gross the minimum threshold to file taxes quite easily. It's always a good idea to get clarification from an accountant when it comes to filing your taxes, so that you make sure it's all done correctly and nothing is overlooked.

If you plan to make a good yearly salary from your blogging, you will naturally need to pay taxes on that income. There are also deductions that you can take. Things you can deduct include any expenses directly related to your blogging. These will include things such as expenses from registering your domain name, blog hosting fees, if you need to hire a tech person to help with your site, purchasing apps and programs that help with the blogging, fees from advertising your blog, and so forth. If you are a full-time blogger, you will have even more expenses that you can deduct, including a home office expense. You can also deduct things like office supply costs, tickets to blogging conferences, books on blogging, and more.

In order for you to deduct these expenses, you will need to keep track of them, just as you do your earned income. Keep the receipts from the payments you make for these things. I keep an envelope in my desk drawer where I put all the expense receipts once I log them into my accounting system. At the end of the year, if you do your taxes, you will need the information regarding what your gross income and net income was. Not only will you need that information when it comes to filing taxes, but you will also want to keep track of it so you know what you are making and spending each year. This gives you the ability to track your growth each year.

LIBEL AND SLANDER

When you write blog posts, there are things you need to be aware of so that you don't cross the line and get into trouble. The words *libel* and *slander* are ones that you need to be familiar with. Slander is saying something about someone that is untrue or damaging. Libel includes such statements that have been published. If you write a scathing blog post about someone and say things that are not true, or say things that will harm their reputation, you may commit libel. People can sue you if they feel you have libeled them.

The internet has opened up a world to the possibilities of libel and defamation. Ever take a look at some of the comments that people make on posts? Those count, too. Many people don't realize that when they comment on social media outlets and say things that are considered libel, they can end up in hot water. It's a good idea to avoid saying negative things about specific people, especially if they are untrue or will damage their reputation, so that you avoid any negative recourse. As a blogger, I have had an experience with this issue.

A couple of years ago, I got a knock on the door and was officially served. I was shocked to read the lawsuit that was before me. Along with my blog, I run a local Facebook page with the same name. I was being sued for posting the link to a news article about something that had gone on in our city *three years prior*. I had no recollection of the incident that this lawsuit was referring to. I had to investigate what it was about and get to the bottom of it.

As it turns out, there was a news story regarding something that had happened in our county three years prior to the lawsuit. I had taken the link to the news article and posted it on my blog's Facebook page, because it was an article that I believed my audience would be interested in. I merely posted the article link, and didn't write anything with it. It was only a link to the news article about the story. I was being sued for doing that, which left me dumbfounded. I never said anything about the person in question, or even commented on the article.

I was not the only person named in the lawsuit. The person was also suing our city council and several parents who had *commented* on the post on my page. At this point, I didn't believe for a second that I had done anything wrong, because I never said anything about the person. How could someone be sued for posting a link to a news article? However, I still had to answer the lawsuit, which required hiring an attorney who is familiar with this type of law.

As it turns out, I was protected by the Communications Decency Act, and the lawsuit was dropped. But this person had claimed that they were unable to get a job in the last three years because of that post, therefore they were suing everyone they thought contributed to it, with the exception of the news outlet that covered the story, of course. Apparently it wasn't what the person had done to make the news that made it difficult to get a job, but it was people finding out about it through social media.

Being a writer, I already knew about such things as libel and slander and have always been aware of such things when writing or posting. However, since that lawsuit, I've become even more cautious. I know that I'm protected and I know what would be considered libel, so I know that I am not doing anything to end up in trouble. But truth be told, I don't want to have to hire another attorney to respond to such things. It cost me time and money and brought undue stress into my life that I just don't need.

Keep these issues in mind when you are writing your blog posts, posting on your social media outlets, and when you are commenting on social media in general. Libel can be an issue in any of these areas if you are writing things that will defame someone or harm their reputation, or if what you are writing is untrue.

DISCLOSURE MATTERS

I have been on many blogs that do not have a disclosure. I always wonder if the blogger doesn't realize they need one or if they are trying to skirt the issue altogether. As a blogger who is earning money from your work, you need to disclose to viewers that you earn from your blog, through payments, affiliate links, etc. A disclosure is going to let your readers know that you have partnerships, revenue streams, and you get some freebies.

This is a requirement by the Federal Trade Commission (FTC). They offer a whole section on their website about endorsement guidelines and disclosures. Their concern comes into play when readers can't tell what you are being paid to promote and what you are promoting simply because you love a product. For example, if you have a review post on a new product that is out and you are promoting it, the FTC wants readers to know if you are being paid to give that good review, or if you received something in order to give it, or if it's a genuine review about a product that you purchased on your own.

If you received a product for free, you don't have to disclose anything to the audience. This is because the FTC says that stores give out free samples, too, so you can receive free samples and give your opinion as well. The FTC is concerned about you being paid to endorse something and not disclosing that to the viewers. Therefore, if you have been paid to promote something, even a guest post or affiliate links, you should disclose this on your site.

You don't have to do anything elaborate to have a disclosure on your blog, but if you are being paid for posts, have affiliate links, or otherwise earn money from your blog, you need to have one on there. This will ensure you are covered and don't get into trouble with the FTC. You can write this as part of your post, such as stating that it's a sponsored post, or you can also have a blanket disclosure for your site. Having a disclosure on your site ensures that your viewers will know that you are receiving payments for things on the site.

Some bloggers, including myself, include a link to a disclosure statement on the bottom of each post. That link takes readers to a disclosure statement that lets them know that there are some paid advertisers and affiliate links, and that I make money from these things. There's no set way you have to let readers know you make money from things on your site, but you have to do it someway, so that they are aware of it and you are in compliance with the FTC.

PRIVACY, COOKIES, AND MORE

Cookies collect information about who visits your blog. You have likely visited other websites where you have to give them an acknowledgment that you are okay with them using cookies. You may need to add a plug-in for this depending on where you live, such as in the United Kingdom, and depending on what type of platform you are using. Check with your blogging platform to see if there is anything you need to do for this.

Many bloggers have a privacy statement published on their site. If you would like to include one, you can find standard templates for them online. Similarly, you can add a policy statement about what you do with email information that is collected, if you do collect email addresses. If you choose to send out email newsletters, for example, you will be collecting viewer email addresses. Some people may be concerned about the privacy and want to know if you plan to sell your contact list or do something else with it, thus giving their information away to others.

These things can be addressed through posted statements. If you will be collecting personal information about people, then you need to have a privacy policy posted. Since you will be using information that has been collected and you will access in your analytics or has been given to advertising networks, such as Google AdSense, it is a good idea to have a privacy policy on your blog.

Another posted statement that some people have on their blog is a terms of service. You can find templates for this online as well. If you plan to allow comments on your blog, then you may want to have a terms of service posted.

This is not a requirement, but some people do it to cover themselves should situations arise that call for it.

If you question whether or not you need some of these things, it's better to err on the side of having the statements posted somewhere on the site so that you are protected. You can find templates for most of these things online and then use them to tailor it to your blog.

COPYRIGHT ISSUES

As a writer, I assume that people know that they cannot simply go copy and paste someone else's article and use it as their own. But I'm often reminded that this is not the case at all. A few years ago, I was loaded with writing work to do. My list of projects was long, which I was grateful for, but at the same time, a business acquaintance contacted me. She said that her writer was looking for some freelance work and she wondered if I had any that I could give to her.

Well, the timing was perfect, so I decided to give her a few articles to write for me to test her out and see how it went. A couple of days went by, and the work was submitted to me and I paid her for it. I then took to making sure that it was original content, rather than something that she had taken from someone else. Lo and behold, the articles *were* merely copied and pasted from articles online. I was disappointed, but not all that shocked.

I went back to my business acquaintance who had sent her to me and I let her know that the work was copied and pasted articles; it was not at all fresh or unique content. She laughed and informed me that it was no big deal, that is what she always does. That is when I became shocked at this situation. As it turns out, that was the standard at her business. I let her know that it was unacceptable that she was doing this, using plagiarized articles, but she didn't think it was an issue. They had been doing it for years, and she laughed it off that it was no big deal.

It really is a big deal. Plagiarism is no joke. If you copy and use someone's work as your own, that is not only unethical, but illegal. Don't pass someone else's work off as yours. Just as work you write is automatically copyrighted, so too is theirs. Now, there are some people who give free rein to use their work as you would like. But those people are few and far between. Most people don't want their work taken and used without permission.

There are some things you can do and still be legal. If someone sends you a press release, you can use that as it is and post it. That's what it is intended for. If you find a fact or quote you want to use, you can use it, but attribute the information to the source. If you are quoting someone, say "according to . . ." so that it doesn't seem as though you are making it your own.

There is what is referred to as "fair use," which allows you to use some material on a limited basis. Fair use allows you to use some content, especially in situations where you may be giving a review or critique of something. This may include a few lines of material, summarizing a quote, and copying a few paragraphs from a news article. If there is content you want to use for something like a review, be sure to check the fair use guidelines first so you don't get yourself into trouble for using content or material that you are not allowed to use.

Material that is considered public domain can be freely used by anyone. You won't have to get permission in order to use the content if it is considered public domain. This is good to know as it pertains to work that is created by government employees. Generally speaking, the work that they create on behalf of the federal government is considered public domain, so you are free to use the information as you would like and don't need to get permission first. Information put out by the federal government that is considered public domain includes most instructional videos, pamphlets, maps, documents, and images. Not all federal government content is considered public domain though, so if there is something you want to use, be sure that it falls under the public domain category before using it.

The same issues for content exist when using images. You can get into trouble for taking someone else's intellectual property. If you see a design or photograph you like online, that doesn't mean you can go use it. You have to get permission, and may have to pay a fee or royalty to do so. There are free images online that you can use, and you can always make your own. Using Canva is a great way to get unique graphics for your blog without infringing on someone else by taking their graphics. You can use free outlets to get images, you can pay a couple of dollars per image when you buy from stock image sites, you can contact people directly to see how they feel about you using their image or design, and you can create your own. You can also take a lot of pictures yourself and use your own work online.

You may find that you write unique content that someone else comes along and uses without your permission. As soon as you wrote and published your work, it was legally copyrighted, so others should not take it without your permission. If you do find someone using it, they will usually remove it if you contact them and ask them to do so. This is unless you don't mind some others using your articles. One of the most popular bloggers, Zen Habits, has made all of his written work public domain. He lets people know that they are free to use his work. He appreciates attribution, but doesn't require it.

REMAINING LEGAL

There are things you need to be aware of in order to stay legal as a blogger. Sometimes those things change or new legal issues may arise. It's a good idea to try to keep up on what legal issues emerge so that you can be prepared. Don't let the legal side of blogging overwhelm you. You want to stay compliant, but it's honestly a small portion of your time that will go to doing so.

There is an initial investment in time to get things set up legally, but once you do, then you won't have to worry about it until there are changes in the industry. As long as you are keeping track of things like your income and expenses, avoiding libel, and using unique content, you will be fine.

Blogging can be a lot of fun, but like any career, there are going to be legal issues that you have to keep in mind. It doesn't matter what kind of career or side job you have that you earn money from—you will have some legal issues to contend with. Don't obsess over them or let them overwhelm you, but do address them to make sure you are covered. You will like the peace of mind knowing that you are protected if an issue should arrive.

BLOGGER SPOTLIGHT
Katie Moseman
Recipe for Perfection
www.recipeforperfection.com

Magnolia Days
www.magnoliadays.com

When did you first start blogging and what got you interested in doing so?
I started blogging in 2014 when I was a stay-at-home mom. I decided to start a blog because I wanted to keep my technology skills current and possibly make some money on the side.

What blogging format do you use, and are you happy with it?

I've used WordPress since the beginning, and I like it. It's not perfect, but it's affordable and customizable without too much trouble.

How long did it take before you were making a good salary each year from your blog?

I completed my first sponsored post about six months after starting my blog. It took about a year for any income to become steady. At first, I earned a few hundred dollars per month via sponsored posts; eventually, I gained enough traffic to make money from display ads as well.

What did you find to be your biggest challenge in blogging, and how did you overcome it?

The biggest challenge in blogging was to decide how to spend my time. Do you focus on social media? Do you spend time and money on SEO? What about producing videos? I still struggle to balance everything, but experience has taught me to hold off on running after fads. I stick to what I'm good at and I focus on that: good photography, solid on-page SEO, and the repurposing of blog content into books.

What advice would you offer to new bloggers, or those who are still struggling to earn money from their blog?

Learn SEO first. Otherwise, you'll make lots of mistakes you'll have to fix later. Find your topic and become an authority on it. It's not always necessary to have a "niche," but it is necessary to focus on a handful of areas that form a coherent brand. My blog Recipe for Perfection contains simple recipes with straightforward directions and helpful tips for less-experienced cooks. My blog Magnolia Days focuses on Southern life with an emphasis on food and travel.

What is one thing you have done that has helped you be able to earn more blogging?

Write with the reader in mind. My blogging motto is "Be helpful." Solve problems. You can do this and still align your writing with what you're interested in.

What is your top tip for bloggers who want to earn a salary from their blog?

Set up multiple revenue streams so that your earnings are steady. When one flags, you'll have others to rely on. For example: I earn money from sponsored posts, display ads, and books I publish on Amazon. Some bloggers even sell their services, like photography, videography, graphics, or web design, to other bloggers.

8

Building Your Following

You can blog your heart out, but if nobody reads it then you won't be able to make much money from your efforts. Every successful blog is going to need a following. You need to have people who read it on a regular basis, as well as people who find you in search engines and read pages here and there. In order for anyone to make money from blogging, they need one very important thing—traffic!

I've met with other bloggers who have been at it for months or even a couple of years, and they are frustrated. They see that their blog is not getting any traffic, but they have no idea what they are doing wrong, or what they are simply not doing that is keeping them from getting a flow of traffic to the site. That's when I usually log on to take a look at their blog. From there I can usually see some things they are doing, or not doing, that may be the problem. There are a lot of things that you can do in order to build a following and keep people wanting to come back to your blog.

CONTENT GOALS

One of the most important things you can do to build a following and keep people coming back to your blog is to provide good content. If you are putting out information that people find to be of value to them, they will want to come back. There is no one-size-fits-all when it comes to what people will find of value. This means that you have to know who your target market is. When you have identified your target market, you will have a good idea what type of things they want.

When it comes to blogging, content is king. Whether you are putting out posts that cover fashion, cooking, home repairs, or random thoughts, it doesn't matter. What matters is that you have identified who your target market is and you are writing things that they will want to pay attention to. If someone finds your site for the first time through a search engine, you have seconds to grab their attention and make them want to read more, and make them want to come back again.

If the article they landed on was of interest or value to them, they may go further to take a look at your home page, read a few more articles, perhaps even sign up for your emails or follow you on a social media outlet. If they are not impressed with what they see, they are not likely to do much. They may even leave the site altogether within seconds of landing there.

Think about what it is that makes you want to keep following a blogger. What is it that they do to keep you coming back? My personal favorite blogger is Karen Maezen Miller. She's a Buddhist author who has also written several books that I love. I never miss reading one of her blog posts. Her blog, titled Cheerio Road, speaks to me. The issues that she writes about always touch me in some way. I can relate to them and I take value in the lesson or information that she is providing in them. Her blog posts are clever, heartfelt, and there always seems to be a lesson in there. Those lessons resonate with me. They make me think, they make me look at things differently, and at times I have felt that they spoke to me so much that they were written specifically for me. I know that's not possible, but that's how her posts make me feel.

Her posts have created a connection with me. That connection keeps me wanting to go back and read them. Not only have I made sure I've read all her books, but as soon as a new blog post comes out I get the email for it, and it becomes a priority for me to read the new post.

Consider how many emails you get per day or week that you simply hit the "delete" key on to get rid of. Even for newsletters and websites that you have purposely signed up and told them to go ahead and send you the information. Delete, delete, delete. We remove far more email messages from non-friends than we open and take the time to read. What is it that makes you open the emails that you finally do decide to check out? Those things that make you want to open the email, rather than delete it, and make you want to keep reading the posts are things you want to keep in mind. If those things work to keep you reading, then they will work for others as well.

When you consider what it is that you like that other bloggers or websites do, also think about what you don't like that they do. If there are things that you don't like at all, then you want to be aware of them so you don't do those things on your own blog. There's one thing that I see some sites do and that is to have multiple pages or a slideshow to give you the information you are looking for. For example, they will have a posted titled "10 Amazing Places to Retire in the Southwest." If I click on that, I want to see a list of the places. I don't like when some sites will create a slideshow of the ten places, placing one picture and a line of content on each slide, or span that list out to ten pages. They do this to inflate their page views and keep you on the site longer.

The problem is that, well, the pages are inflated. Their traffic information is going to be overinflated because they made people look at ten slides or pages to see a list of ten places. As a reader, it's really frustrating to sit through that, and I don't care for them inflating their page views and serving me up loads of ads like that. I sat through it a few times, hated it, and decided that was the end of that. Anytime I land on a site now that has such antics, I close right out. I'm not playing that game. Sure, they may overinflated their traffic numbers some, but they have turned off readers. It's not a good trade-off, if you ask me.

Since I don't like that style as a reader, I would never want to do that to my readers. The things you like and dislike about other people's sites can help guide you when creating your own content. Posting content that you would like and posting it in a way that you like to read it will help to ensure that your readers like it as well.

CONSISTENCY COUNTS

In order to build a following, you need to blog consistently. Now, as mentioned in a prior chapter, there is no set number of times per day, week, or month that you need to publish a post. But you do need to do it with some consistency. My favorite blogger, mentioned above, only publishes two to three blog posts per month. That number works for her, as it does me. If she blogged daily I would probably grow less interested in it over time. If her blog posts seemed to say the same thing over and over I'd also probably grow less interested. I used to have another favorite blog, which I won't mention the name of, that I grew less interested in over time. This is because it seemed like the posts were all becoming the same thing. The person had found maybe three angles that people must have liked and then every post was a rehash of those angles.

You can rehash and expand upon angles some, but if they become all you are publishing then you run the risk of the reader growing weary. I still receive this blogger's emails, but I hit the delete key probably nine out of every ten times. I feel like I already know what the blog post is going to be and I no longer find value in it, because it's the same thing over and over.

If you don't blog enough, you run the risk that your readers will forget who you are and about your blog. This has happened to me a couple of times. I find blogs I like, I sign up to get their emails, and soon they taper off and then stop coming all together. Then one day out of the blue I get an email with the blogger saying "I'm back!" At that point I don't even recall who the person is, so there's no excitement to me that they are back. I took the time to investigate when that happened with one blogger and found that about two years had gone by since they had last sent out a post. As you can imagine, that's simply too much time to pass if you want to build a loyal following.

To earn money as a blogger you have to have a following. In order to have a following you have to consistently put out content that is of value to the readers. It's that simple. I know that people get busy and it's easy to find a laundry list of excuses (which may or may not include doing the laundry), but you must make blogging a part of your schedule. If you feel your schedule is busy, or if you work a day job as well, then put it on your calendar. Schedule in time that you will work on your blog, even if it's just two hours every Friday night. Get in the habit of blogging regularly. You can get up an hour early every day to blog before work, blog in your car on lunch breaks, or blog a half an hour before bed each night. Do whatever works for you, as long as you find a way to consistently blog, because that's the only way you can build a following, grow your blog, and earn a salary from it.

SOCIAL MEDIA

Bloggers can use social media outlets to build a following. However, it's important to make sure you are using the ones for your target market. If you are not, then you will likely not be all that successful in finding your readers. Know the demographics of who typically uses the social media platform you are considering investing time into using to promote your blog.

Once you narrow down which social media platforms you want to use to help build your platform, focus on what you are going to post to them. The last thing people want is for you to constantly try to sell them something. If you do that, they will merely hit the unlike or unfollow button. Trying to consistently sell things to your audience is one quick way to turn them off. Even if you do have products to sell, you have to be more subtle about what you are offering. Post after post trying to sell them something will not build your blog a following.

It's important to post things that will be of value, or that that they find interesting, humorous, or that they can relate to. If you are using a platform that gives them a chance to comment, such as Facebook, ask them a question so there's interaction. That's what social media is all about. It's not just you posting whatever you want, it's a social outlet where people get to comment and interact with one another.

One thing that I must warn you about when it comes to using social media is that it's given people a license to be rude. You have likely seen this among your own personal social media pages, but until you are running your own pages and post things to see it firsthand, you just don't realize how rude people can be. Social media has given people a way to socialize more, but certainly not socialize better. People feel bold and anonymous online and they tend to say things online that they would never say to your face.

I warn you of this because if you have a large enough following on social media pages you will experience ugly behavior from some readers. I have over 33,000 followers for my local blog. No matter what I post there will always be some people who comment with something rude. I could post a picture of the beautiful blue sky outside and within seconds I'll get a couple of people who will have something negative to say about it. It never fails. I've even tested it before and it doesn't matter how positive the thing that you post, there are Negative Nellys, as I call them, that will always comment on your thread.

When you deal with the public being a blogger and using social media to build a following, you have to grow a thick skin. If you are not interacting with your audience or not that active on social media you likely won't have to worry about this, but if you are active and have a large audience, be prepared. You can't let it bring you down. Some of the people will say mean things that make you wonder why you are doing what you do. But you have to learn to ignore that type of behavior and keep pushing on. As long as the majority of your audience is interacting in a good way, don't focus on the one or two Negative Nellys who try to bring your thread or post down.

In *The Art of Social Media: Power Tips for Power Users*, author Guy Kawasaki says, "If you're not pissing someone off on social media, you're not using it aggressively enough." While I don't suggest purposely trying to make people mad, remembering this quote may help make you feel better once you do.

SHOW YOUR PERSONALITY

What is it that sets bloggers apart from any other regular websites on the internet? It's personality! When you read articles that are published on other websites, you usually get straightforward, here-is-the-information type of pieces. You get your standard article written either to conform to a journalistic style or you get one that merely presents the information, quotes an expert or three, and then offers you a solution to whatever problem it is that you are experiencing and the piece is covering. There's no personality, which means there is no way to make a connection.

When it comes to bloggers, we can and should share our personality and lives in our posts. That's what makes us bloggers, rather than straight content writers. When you infuse your personality into your blog, you will build a following that connects to your personality. Your audience will like who you are. They even come to feel like they know you, even if they have never met you before. If they ever do meet you in person, they will automatically feel you are a friend from afar. I've had people tell me this, because they got to know me so well through my blog.

Let your personality shine through on your blog. That is what sets you apart, and people who enjoy your content will feel a connection to you. It's a good way to help build a following. People don't just follow a blog for the information on the posts; they also follow the blog because they like the blogger.

COMMENTS GALORE

Comments can be a great way to interact with your readers. It gives them a chance to add on to something you have blogged about, ask you a question, or provide feedback. You can also then respond back to the people. Comments can be a tool for connecting with your audience. But they can become a problem, too.

Personally, I hate comments on the blog. I made this decision years ago and it led to me to set my site up to where the comments section only stays open on a post for one week, then it automatically closes. I don't like to get comments on my blog. I do realize that some bloggers love it, but that's not me.

I found comments to be both time-consuming and too filled with spam. What happens is that you think you will get your readers comment to say something or ask a question. But that's not what usually happens. Instead, you get loads of people who write something that is often obscure or may not even pertain to what you wrote about. They do this because their blog or website link gets posted to your site along with their comment. This gives their site a backlink, and as mentioned earlier, backlinks are helpful to your site's ranking.

With the comments section left open you can expect a lot of spam, or people who are looking to promote their own site by commenting on yours. If you like that kind of thing, then more power to you, by all means let it fly. But I don't like it at all. I don't blog to give a platform for spammers or self-promoters to come along and post links to their website. I grew tired of that happening and decided to change my comment default settings.

Not only do my comments sections only stay open for a week, but I also have it set to where I have to approve of all comments before they post. This way, if someone leaves a comment on my blog I will see that when I log into my blogging dashboard, and I can choose to publish or delete it. I can also mark it as spam. Typically speaking, I don't publish it and reply to those that are not spam. Instead, I reply to the person via email.

If someone legitimately has a question, comment, or concern, I'm happy to communicate with them about it. Only I do it through email instead of in the comments section of the blog. While I don't like blog comments, due to repeat spam issues, I have no problem with interacting with my readers in other ways. I have made it easy for people to communicate with me. They can email me directly or they can message me through my blog's Facebook page. I try to respond to every inquiry I receive and it's worked fine thus far.

I'm not saying you should not allow comments, but I do think it's something you should monitor to see if it's worth the time or brings value to your site. If you are getting spammers who want to promote their own site, then it may be time to rethink the idea of comments. Another issue that I see on other people's blogs is that I will come across an evergreen post, so the information is still relevant to me. However, I will see in the comments from the discussion taking place that the article was written eight years prior. That makes me feel like I'm reading outdated information and sets me on a path to go find another article somewhere on the topic.

Comments can really date your blog, letting people know how old your posts are. Speaking of the topic, some bloggers choose to leave the dates on their blog posts, having it set up to post the date for the readers to see. This is a controversial topic in the blogging world. Some insist that the date stamp should be on there, while others prefer to remove them. I've read thoughts on both side of the issue, but nothing has convinced me to want to leave the date on each post. I prefer to rely upon my own experience with running blogs.

There's no right or wrong answer here so you will have to make the decision for yourself which route you prefer. You can always try it one way for a while and then change it if you prefer. Your decision is not set in stone.

I personally prefer to not default to show the date that it was published. This way the posts, as they become older, don't seem old to the reader if they stumble across one where the information is still relevant. If I do want the reader to know about something that is date-specific, I will be sure to write that in my post so the reader has a time frame of when the post was published. When I'm a reader of blogs I also prefer there not be a date stamp. I can't tell you how many times I come across a blog post and lose interest as soon as I see it is years old. Doesn't matter what the topic is, I assume there is more updated and relevant information available somewhere. Without the date stamp, I'd continue to read and wouldn't question if the information is outdated.

The important thing is to find ways to communicate with your readers, whether it is through responding to comments, replying to emails, through social media, or in person at events. It's a great way to make a connection and create loyal readers. Not everyone has to use the same methods to communicate with their readers. You can do what you are comfortable with and what you feel works best for you.

EMAIL COMMUNICATION

Sending out emails to readers was discussed in chapter 4, as a way to help promote your blog. Emails can help also build a following. Many bloggers will give something away to get people to sign up for their email. This gives them an opportunity to have contact with the reader. The item you give away can be a free e-book, list of tips, set of recipes, whatever it is that you feel will interest your audience.

Once people sign up to receive that freebie, you will have their contact information, and you will be able to reach out to them again by sending out an email. You will need to play around with your email system to see what works best for you in terms of the types of headlines that get more people to open the email, and what types of links people will click on. Keep in mind what was discussed in chapter 4, however, regarding how many email newsletters simply go to spam. This can be problematic if you are collecting the contact information and then not seeing much action when you send out a newsletter or message.

I have seen some bloggers use a variety of routes to grow their email list and social media pages. Some of them I don't believe are helpful to their overall goal of connecting with their audience or in growing the traffic to their blog. How can this be? Well, let me give you a couple of examples that I have seen. One local site ran a contest where people vote on the best pictures that were submitted by readers. In order to vote you have to register your email address, or if it's on social media you have to like their page. Those who have entered a photo will get their friends and family members to vote for them, no matter where they live. At the end of the contest you will have gained a lot more likes by default, but they are not at all your target market and won't add to the growth of your blog.

Likewise, if you run a giveaway or contest that requires people to register their email address on your site in order to vote or be entered, that doesn't mean you will help to build your following. Many of the people will who enter their email address to vote for family and friends will not be your target market. At the end, you have grown your email contact list, but not with quality addresses. You have merely skewed your numbers to make it look like you have a lot of people you email. Your emails will go out to people who are not your target market and will be unlikely to open, or click to visit your blog. If they take the time to do so, they will unsubscribe or unfollow you once the contest or giveaway is over. Others will just hit the delete key. Either way, you want quality, not quantity.

Focus your efforts on building your following of people who like your blog and want more information from you. You want people who find value in what you post, not a list of email address of people who were simply voting for Uncle Joe's drawing in a contest for which they were forced to provide their email address in order to cast their vote. It's better to have a smaller email list made up of people who want your newsletter or emails than it is a large list of people who really don't have interest in your blog.

GROUPS, EVENTS, AND MORE

There are additional ways you can build your following and make a connection with your target audience. Join online groups that pertain to your topic. This gives you a chance to connect with people who are looking to discuss topics related to your blog. You can attend events and conferences that pertain to your blog topic as well.

There are events, seminars, and conferences all over the place and all year long. Once you establish your blog and have a following, you can become a speaker at these. Until that time comes, attend them so you can find others who have similar interests. You may even meet other bloggers who cover similar topics, and you can work together to do guest posts on each other's blogs, helping with blog promotion.

Depending on the type of blog you have, you may also be able to host events yourself. These events will give you a chance to invite your readers and followers to attend, where you will be able to make a connection with them. This gives you the platform to meet some of them, have some fun, and give them an in-person experience with your blog, so it kind of brings it to life.

There are many ways you can build a following with your readers. Get creative, try different things, and see what works for you. What works for one person's blog and audience may not resonate with another. It's all about finding what works for you and then taking steps to stick with it to help it grow.

BLOGGER SPOTLIGHT
Shalee Blackmer
Shalee Wanders
www.shaleewanders.com

When did you first start blogging and what got you interested in doing so?
I began my blog at the beginning of 2014 after a lot of my social media friends were interested in how I found flight deals and traveled on a budget. I come from a tiny rural town, so traveling as much as I did wasn't that common. I quickly found myself answering a lot of questions in my inbox about travel, so I decided on a whim to start a travel blog in the hope of inspiring someone to take a trip.

What blogging format do you use, and are you happy with it?
I work through WordPress, which I love, and write mainly travel tips and travel guide blogs. It's my most natural form of writing, and my readers seem to react well to those styles as well.

How long did it take before you were making a good salary each year from your blog?

I made my first decent paycheck off my blog in 2016. Blogging has never been my full-time income because I have never chosen to pursue that career path. However, blogging has opened many opportunities for me. It's launched my career in freelance writing and photography. Beyond that, blogs are great résumés. It elevates me from other candidates when being scouted by project managers and in the overall job market.

What did you find to be your biggest challenge in blogging, and how did you overcome it?

When I started my blog, I was still in college and balancing two jobs. I didn't give myself the proper time to invest in it. This was okay for at first, but as my readership grew, and I realized my blog was becoming more than just a hobby, I struggled to keep up. My unpreparedness lost me a lot of opportunities, but eventually, I found a balance and a schedule that worked for me and stuck to it.

When you start a blog, dedication and the ability to work on your own are the keys to success. No one is going to tell you to sit down and write or edit photos. You have to learn how to fit it into your schedule.

What advice would you offer to new bloggers, or those who are still struggling to earn money from their blog?

Be patient and invest time in learning search engine optimization (SEO). Blogging isn't a new concept anymore, and there are tens of thousands of blogs on the internet competing for the same spot and the same readers. If you start a blog today, don't expect to make income next month. It takes time to establish your credibility and for brands to understand you're serious about the business. Search engine optimization is the fancy term for how visible you are online. Are you ranking on search engines? Are you optimizing your website? If you don't know the answer to these questions, it's time to start learning how SEO can impact your blog.

What is one thing you have done that has helped you be able to earn more blogging?

My secret blogging sauce is photography. We live in a visual world, which means we can't just write a blog anymore and get away with it. People want visual stimulation. And these photos can't just be photos; they need to be good photos. Investing in photography launched my blogging and my success to a whole new level.

What is your top tip for bloggers who want to earn a salary from their blog?

Be different. Anyone can create a blog, which makes it vital to ensure yours is unique and tells your own story. There are a million other travel, wellness, and fitness bloggers out there. What's your story? Why should people read your content over your competitors? Your personality is your most prominent part of your brand. Showcase it! If you frame your entire blog off someone else's blogging success, you lose authenticity and struggle to find the market that genuinely represents who you are.

9

Ways to Enhance Your Blog

When it comes to how blogs look and what type of bells and whistles they offer, they run the gamut. I've been to blogs that are clean, with very little going on across the page, and I've been to blogs where the complete opposite is true. The things you do to enhance your blog are all up to you and they are personal preferences. You can always try some things out to see what you like. If you don't like some of the enhancements you can always ditch them, usually with ease.

Some of the things you do to enhance your blog will be for your reader's benefit, while others may be for your own. If you feel that enhancing your blog with various features adds value, then you should give it a try. You may try some enhancements and discover that they are not worth the time, effort, space, or tech support that goes into them.

Whether you use them or not, it's a good idea to know what type of options are out there to help you enhance your blog. There are more things that come along each year, so if you don't see something that suits your needs here, just wait, because it may end up available before you know it.

ADD A PROFILE PAGE

I don't know about you, but I always want to know who is behind the blog I'm looking at. I want to put a face with the voice, and if I like the blog (or sometimes if I don't like the blog), I want to be able to know a little about the blogger. A blog should have an "about me" page on it, where you let readers know who you are. Share a little information with the readers about yourself, why you are blogging on that topic, what inspires you, etc.

There's no set information you have to provide, but readers like to know who the blogger is, so let them know. Also, include a picture of yourself.

As a reader, I want to see who the blogger is, and there's a good chance you will want to as well. If I come across a blog that doesn't have this information, I am a little leery wondering why, and I think it detracts from the site. It's hard to make a connection to a blogger or become a loyal fan when I don't know who the person is behind it.

Adding a profile page on your blog is not time-consuming at all, and it's free to do so. With that in mind, I can't think of any downsides to letting people know who you are. If you don't want people to know your last name or be able to find you demographically, you can always skip putting your last name on there. There are ways to let readers know who you are without giving away lot of personal information.

PHOTOGRAPHY SKILLS

Blogs usually have photographs on them. Whether it's one photo per blog post or more, the photographs you use can make a big difference. While you can purchase stock photography or use free images that are online, it's nice if you have some photography skills for taking your own photos. I know how important this is, because it's something I severely lack, and I see great photography on other people's blogs.

Not long ago, I purchased a good camera. That was my first attempt toward moving closer to improving my photography skills. I want to be better with the photos I take for my blog, I just need to learn how to do it. Since I bought the camera I have practiced with it a lot. I have even read a couple of photography books that explain how to take good photos. Truth be told, I still stink at it. I can go to my son's soccer match and take a hundred shots, think they will be amazing, and get home and load them onto my computer only to see that three are decent. Decent. Not even good.

I have come to the conclusion that in order for me to grasp being a better photographer, I'm going to have to take a class. I know that better photography on my blogs is something I want, but it's a skill that I lack currently, therefore I need some training.

I was at a food event with other bloggers over a year ago. The restaurant had invited a dozen bloggers that cover different genres in the area to come and be treated to a bunch of food and learn about the restaurant. I pulled out my cell phone to take photos of the food for my blog, with half of them coming out blurry, of course. Other bloggers at the table pulled out nice professional looking cameras and got serious about the photos they took for their blogs. I want to be like them. You may want to as well. Great photographs never hurt, and will always enhance.

COPYWRITING SKILLS

I came into blogging already being a writer, so that part came naturally for me. Many people, however, do not find writing to be natural for them. They may even struggle at it, as I do with the photography. Good copywriting skills can help enhance your blog. When you have good writing skills, your articles are better organized, written more for the reader's ease, and you will know how to write good headlines.

You don't have to be a writer or have a writing background to become a blogger. But if you find that you struggle with it, then you may want to consider improving your skills in that area. You can read some books on copywriting, and you can also consider taking a class that teaches you some writing skills. Classes of this kind be found online and in person. Your local community college may offer copywriting or other types of writing classes, as well as some of your local art hubs.

USING VIDEO

Video can be a fun and interesting way to enhance your blog. Some bloggers have both written content and videos on their blog, and some people are strictly vloggers (video bloggers). My son is a vlogger. He has a YouTube soccer channel where he creates all soccer-related videos to post, but they are also put on his blog (TristansSoccerReviews.com). At thirteen, he has better video-making skills that I do. He takes video and then uses Camtasia on my computer to edit and turn them into something that people enjoy watching.

YouTube has made it more difficult in recent years for people to make money being vloggers. In order to be allowed to put ads on your videos and earn from them you have to have at least a thousand subscribers, and at least four thousand hours of your videos watched within the last year. For someone who is new it can take a while for you to reach this point, where you can begin earning money from your videos. If you want to be a vlogger, or be a blogger who also has videos, have patience. If you have patience and keep working at it, then you should reach those figures and be able to start earning money. There are plenty of vloggers and bloggers who make money from their videos.

Even if you have no intention of being a vlogger, you may still want to enhance a few blog posts with videos you take. I have a nature blog where I write about places to hike and the natural springs in Florida. I will usually take a video when I'm out there exploring. I write up a lengthy blog post with the information about the place, I include numerous pictures, and I also like to include a video. People love videos, so I have them covered when I include one. I post the video on YouTube and then embed the code into the blog post. If someone finds my video on YouTube, rather than finding my blog post first, then they will also see in the description that they can visit my nature blog for more information on the place.

Again, the same holds true with videography as with photography and copywriting skills. If you don't have these skills and feel that you want them, learn the trade. Investing in courses to learn how to do something will usually be worth the return on investment. Using those skills to enhance your blog will make it better, and better blogs tend to have more of a following, which helps the blogger earn more money.

PLUG-INS AND SEARCHES

Depending on the type of blogging format you use, there are many plug-ins that you can use to enhance your blog. Plug-ins are pieces of software code that will help your blog to do something. Some may track users, gather demographic information, help people be able to read documents, give you customization tools, build your email list, add security protection, speed up your website, and more. There are many options you can choose from.

If you are interested in using plug-ins, you can search around online to read about the many different kinds and what they are used for. Some of the plug-ins are free, while others require a fee to use. You have to determine which ones make sense for your blog and if you want to use them. Using them also depends on the blogging platform you use.

As a Typepad user, I don't really use plug-ins. Most available plug-ins are for use with platforms like WordPress. Having said that, I did have one WordPress blog that I did with two other bloggers as a collaboration. Several plug-ins were used on that blog. One of the things I didn't like was that things can go wrong with the plug-ins—and did. When something happens to the plug-ins, such as if they didn't update properly, it can shut your blog down. Not only did that happen to us, but we had to hire a tech person to fix the issues. Using Typepad since 2009, this is something I wasn't used to having to do and didn't care for the additional expenses. This is not to say that you shouldn't use plug-ins. Millions of people do use them and I'm sure are happy with them.

One thing I do have on my blogs is a search tool. I want people to have the ability to search my blog for what they are looking for. I use the one provided through my Google AdSense account, so that it also gives me an opportunity to earn more money. People can do searchers on my blog and Google will search my site for things that are a good fit, but they will also give the person some ads at the top of the results list. If the person clicks on the ads, I earn money.

CUSTOM LOGO AND DESIGN

Having a custom logo on your site is going to enhance it and give it some personality. Whether your blog is your personal name or it is called something else, you can easily have a custom logo made that will jazz the blog up. You can pay someone to create a professional logo, you can use online logo-creating software, or you can create it yourself using Canva.

If you hire someone to create your logo, you will provide them with a few ideas you have, so they know what you like in terms of colors and have a little direction to go in. They will usually come back and show you a few options and you can choose from there to use it the way it is or have them make additional custom changes. I have logos that I have a graphic designer create, usually costing me no more than fifty dollars. You can find graphic designers for this type of thing through a site like Guru.com.

Having your own custom logo makes you look more professional, it adds character to your blog, and it helps to brand your blog name. When I first launched my local blog in 2009, Volusia County Moms, I had a logo professionally created. I loved it and have stuck with it ever since. Over the years I have had several people try to convince me to change my logo. I've even had graphic artists create a logo for me in hopes that I would like it and want to make the switch. While I like some of the new proposed designs I've seen, I still don't want to switch. I like the logo I have and I've spent over a decade using it as part of my branding.

If you hire a website designer or tech person you can also have some custom options done to your blog. Custom features can go a long way toward enhancing it to look unique and speak to your target market. If you are not already doing so, you should also always have your blog using its own direct

URL, not an extension of your blog platform's URL. For example, you want www.yourwebsite.com and not www.yourwebsite.wixsites.com. Using a host's platform keeps your website from looking professional and it makes it difficult for people to type in the URL to find your website easily.

MEDIA KIT

In order to make some money from your blogging it helps to have either a media kit or a page on your site that offers similar information. A media kit is something used in the advertising and marketing world. It would include what a potential advertiser would want to know if they were looking over your blog and considering advertising on it. Include such information as your demographics, page view statistics, average monthly users, etc.

In your media kit you are essentially selling your blog as a place for them to advertise. Consider what you would say to them if you were face-to-face, trying to sell them on the idea of advertising on your blog. Why would they want to advertise on your blog? What makes your blog a better fit than somewhere else, such as in print or in Google Ads? Let them know what makes your blog unique, who your audience is, and what they can expect from being on your blog.

Whether they download the media kit or it's all on one page on your blog, this gives potential advertisers a place to go to learn more. You can also link it to a page of testimonials from advertisers, or include them somewhere on the page. This way they can see what other advertisers have to say about their experience being on your site. If you don't have testimonials you can easily get them. Find advertisers of yours that are happy with the results they get on your blog and ask them if they would mind writing a short testimonial for you. I've never had someone say no to this request. They are usually happy to provide the feedback for you.

Having a media kit or page for potential advertisers also gives you something to take with you, should you have in-person meetings with potential advertisers. I've been to numerous meetings with those interested in advertising, and this gives me a chance to offer them some information about the blog. It's nice to have the info, as well as something to leave behind with them. On that same note, you should invest in business cards with your blog name and contact information. This way you can give those out to potential advertisers, those you network with, or anyone else where the topic may come up. Business cards are a really affordable marketing tool that you can order right online.

ADD OTHER BLOGGERS

This idea is one that may not work for everyone. Some blogs will do well adding other bloggers, and for others it may not make sense to do so. Adding other bloggers to your blog will enhance it by bringing more ideas, posts, readers, and depth. If you consider this idea, you do want to be selective who you bring on to add posts on your blog, and you want to have some guidelines for the bloggers to follow.

Having additional regular contributing bloggers will bring your site additional traffic, and may even bring in more revenue. Your next question will be whether or not you should pay the bloggers who are contributing to your blog. This is something only you can decide, because you know your financial situation. If your blog is not making money yet, however, then it won't be a good move to start taking out of your pocket to pay other bloggers to contribute.

You should be able to find others who will contribute who may want to promote their own product or service. This is a good exchange, because you get the benefit of having contributors, and they get the benefit of promoting their business or service. In this case, they would write the blog posts, and then they would have a short one- to two-line bio at the bottom that will provide a link to their own website. This route is different than the one-off guest post solicitations that you will likely be inundated with after a while, because these are ongoing contributors.

ADDITIONAL ENHANCEMENT OPTIONS

Having buttons or links that allow people to start following you on social media easily or share your posts there can help drive traffic to your site. Many people who read a post they like may not think to share it, but when you have the buttons there it puts the idea in their head and it simplifies the action.

Your blog should also be responsive. What that means is the formatting will work well for any type of device that someone tries to view it on. You may have a favorite or common way that you access websites, but that doesn't mean that's what everyone else uses. I tend to split my time by device. During the day I'm mostly on my desktop, accessing websites through there. But after work hours I use my phone more often. I read lots of news stories on my phone.

If the template you choose for your blog is not already responsive, then you may want to consider changing to one that is. Alternatively, you can hire a tech person to make the adjustments for you, or research how to make the changes yourself to make that happen. A while back, Google had warned the internet world that their websites would need to be responsive. If you want your website to be mobile friendly, which will help with your search engine ranking, then it has to be responsive.

Lastly, you may want to consider having a resource or recommendation page. Many bloggers offer this type of page on their blog. It's one page where you put a list of things you recommend. They are typically related to the theme of your blog, of course. You would let readers know that the things on that page are your favorite products or services. The links on that page can link to individual blog posts where you review those items, or they can link right to the company—that is up to you.

One of the beautiful things about having a resource or recommendation page is that you can earn money from that page. When potential advertisers see that you offer such a page they may want to pay you to be included. You can also affiliate link your favorite products on this page and earn from them if people click through and make a purchase. This can help you earn more money from your blog. Just be sure to watch the wording and to provide a disclosure so that your readers know you are earning money from those links and recommendations, if you are earning from them.

Blogs are easy to start and with some patience and persistence you will grow the number of posts you have. With that your traffic should increase and you will be able to earn money from your efforts. If you have been blogging for a while and you are not yet earning a decent income from it, then it's time to seriously evaluate what is holding you back. You may even want to get a second opinion from a more established blogger. Perhaps there are glaring omissions that are holding you back that you don't see, but someone else will notice right away.

Blogging is a great way to earn passive income as well as have a career that pays well if that is the route you want to choose. There are many things you can do to enhance your blog and make it more user friendly and lucrative. Those things may change over time, so be willing to adapt a little as technology changes. If you are willing to go with the flow and make the necessary adjustments, you can have your blog for a long time. Some people even grow a successful blog that is making money and then sell the whole thing to someone else. This gives them one large lump sum of cash, rather than receiving a salary each year from it.

There are many options that exist in the blogging world. The important thing is to get started if you haven't already, or to move past the rut you are in if you are stalled on your current blog. You may have a successful blog already and be reading this as well. I always feel that if I read a book and get one useful piece of information out of it that helps me be more successful, then it was worth reading. So hopefully you get at least one useful piece of information out of this one that will help you become more successful as a blogger and earn more money.

BLOGGER SPOTLIGHT
Joanne Greco
Life with Joanne
www.lifewithjoanne.com

When did you first start blogging and what got you interested in doing so?
I started blogging in 2004. I had adopted three children (siblings) through foster care in 2003 and started unschooling them in 2004. I wanted to share my experiences and connect with other families in similar situations so I created an adoption forum and then a blog.

What blogging format do you use, and are you happy with it?
I use self-hosted WordPress and I am very happy with it. It's made for blogging.

How long did it take before you were making a good salary each year from your blog?
I didn't start monetizing my blog until about 2007. I started as an Amazon affiliate (which I still am) and also used AdSense ads (which I no longer use). It wasn't until around 2011 that I began to create a plan to earn a more constant income from my blog.

What did you find to be your biggest challenge in blogging, and how did you overcome it?
For me, that would be finding time to devote to all the different aspects of blogging. And no, I haven't overcome it yet. Over the last few years, my children have each turned eighteen and I planned on devoting more

time to blogging. Two years ago I received custody of my three-year-old grandson and four-year-old granddaughter, so once again, my time is not my own. Outsourcing has helped and I have several go-to people in certain areas that I trust. But there are times I have to realize I can't do it all and that's okay. Everything doesn't *have* to get done. That's been hard for me but I'm getting there.

What advice would you offer to new bloggers or those who are still struggling to earn money from their blog?

Be patient. If you're new at blogging chances are you need to build an audience first. That takes time. Focus more on what you bring to the table and get better at it. Depending on how you want to make money from your blog, you have to earn the trust of your readers first.

After you've done that (or while you're doing it), start pitching brands with your collaboration ideas. I suggest starting small, maybe even reach out to some local businesses. Also, check your most viewed posts and figure out ways to expand on it. Possible connecting with a sponsor for a follow-up post or adding affiliate links.

What is one thing you have done that has helped you be able to earn more blogging?

Developing genuine friendships with other bloggers. It's helped in a couple of ways. In the early years, it gave me the confidence to keep going and get better at blogging. Later on, the networking, feedback, and the sharing of resources with each other has provided to be invaluable. Don't be afraid to reach out! Join blogging groups, like ours: BodaciousBloggers.com. But remember, as with your audience, what can you bring to the table? Share your knowledge freely and help those who come up after you.

What is your top tip for bloggers who want to earn a salary from their blog?

Don't let anyone tell you that you can't make money if you're a small blogger. The key is your audience. Hone in on what they want and develop a connection with them. That's priceless.

10

Where Your Blog Can Take You

Whether you realize it when you first launch your blog or not, it can actually lead to a lot of other things. These may be paid gigs, as well as nonpaid ones. It can lead you to getting more involved in your community, within the field that your blog covers, and in other ways. A blog can be the platform that opens doors in numerous directions.

SEMINARS AND CONFERENCES

Once I started my blogs, it wasn't long before I started getting invitations to do things like speak at conferences, engage in community activities, and help host events. In fact, I never expected this to happen and wasn't seeking these kinds of opportunities. Many people love things like that and will jump at the chance to get involved. The introvert and writer in me is content to connect with people through my blogs and writing, rather than in person at large functions.

Even being a social introvert, meaning that I can socialize just fine with others, I still prefer to spend most of my time alone. And I'm not a fan of big groups or busy places. I know this about myself and tend to stick to smaller functions, keep a very small group of friends, and love working from a home office where I can toil away on my writing and blogs without others around. Being that type of person, I turned down most of the invitations that I received.

There were a few invitations that I accepted, with hesitation, and wondering if I were nuts on the way to them, but I saw them through. I was a presenting speaker at a marketing conference, teaching people about how to increase social media engagement. I was a guest speaker at a business event, where I gave a presentation on blogging, sharing with people how to get started and how they can use a blog to help bring in more business. There have been other things here and there I have agreed to do as well, but I've passed on most, because it just doesn't fit my personality. But it may be the perfect fit for yours.

There are many seminars and conferences that take place around the country, as well around the world, every year. If this area interests you, blogging can open the door to you getting speaking and workshop engagements. Many of these arrangements will pay you to participate, as well as provide you with travel accommodations or pay for them. Your blog, once you grow it and the traffic, helps to establish you as an expert in the topic your blog is about. You can use that to speak on that topic at events, seminars, workshops, and conferences.

Your blogging may also lead you to offering your own online webinars and summit. Many people are doing this today. Let's say you have a blog that is all about yoga. You could put together an online webinar for yoga instructors, or a summit for those who want to learn all about yoga. You can collaborate with other yoga professionals to put together the summit, with it offering talks on a variety of issues related to yoga. Once that online summit is created, people pay to access it, and it will be promoted by everyone who is contributing to it. There's no expiration either, so this will create a passive income, as it sits there allowing people to pay to access it for years to come. If it does well, you may want to create a new one every year, featuring different experts and updated information to keep people up on the latest in that field.

SELLING PRODUCTS

Let's say you love handbags, so you start a blog that is all about handbags. The blog grows and gets a lot of traffic, because there are millions of other people who love handbags, too. You start making money from advertisers on the site and in other various ways, but then you get an idea that perhaps you could start selling handbags, too.

Blogging is a natural progression to selling something, some kind of product that relates to what your blog is about. No matter what type of blog you have, there are always products that you can sell that will relate to it. You can create your own product, or become a distributor for someone else's products. Your blog may lead to another business opportunity.

There are many businesses that use blogs to bring in more traffic to their site so they can try to sell their products and services. But on the flip side, there are bloggers who start out focused on the blog and find that it leads them to other avenues. One of those avenues is in teaching courses on the blog topic. Whether it's baking amazing wedding cakes, how to sew your own clothes, or how to have an incredible workout before 5:00 a.m., there is a market for it.

Teachable is one of the leading sites that makes it simple for you to create online courses to teach what you know. There are people who have courses on watercolor, using Photoshop to create digital scrapbooks, how to make fabulous cakes, how to freedive, and much more. Once your blog is getting traffic and has a following, you may be drawn to creating a class that offers people an online course that they will pay for.

As the blog grows and you have a following, you will begin to have an automatic audience for the courses you will offer. Once you progress to offering the courses, your blog can naturally be used to help promote them. You can also offer courses in person. Check your local community centers for a place where you can hold your own courses. Where I live, there is a local art center where people can offer classes on a wide variety of things, including yoga, art, writing, foreign languages, and more.

There are so many opportunities to put what you know to use beyond the blog. You may not see them when you first start, but they will emerge as time goes on. If you are writing about families, you can always hold events or workshops that will benefit families. If you are writing about ghost towns in your state, you can speak on that topic, or you can create a product that you can sell to your readers based on that topic.

Books are another possible place that your blog can take you. If you have a following, then you have a platform of people whom you can try to sell your book to. You can write and sell books based on the topic, going more in depth than you would on the blog. Some bloggers, once they have a compilation of blog posts, take those and then turn them into a book. I'm not a big fan of that, because the few books I've read like that seem disjointed, and I feel like I'm reading a series of blog posts, rather than a book. I also feel like I wasted my money, because I could have gone to their blog and read it all for free, rather than purchasing the posts in a book format.

There are plenty of opportunities for writing books that relate to the theme of your blog. You can send these ideas out to traditional publishers and pitch the idea to them. There are also many people who choose to self-publish books today. If you are interested in writing books based on the theme of your blog, do some research regarding the process involved in pitching editors to go the traditional publishing route, as well as what is involved with self-publishing. Once you have done your research on that, you will have an idea as to what route you want to take.

OFFERING SERVICES

Your blog can take you to offering a variety of services, including coaching and writing. Many people like to hire a personal coach today. They can play an important role in helping people to navigate their way to reaching a goal. Whatever your blog theme is, there is likely some coaching opportunities that can follow.

Blogging can also lead you to do more blogging, but for other people. I have shared with you how I have numerous ongoing clients that I blog for. This adds to my yearly salary. When people see that you blog and they like what you are doing, they may be compelled to have you start doing it for them. I have written blog posts for a wide variety of clients over the years, including both businesses and individuals.

The next chapter delves into the idea of blogging for others and goes more in depth into it. If you have interest in your blog leading to you blogging for others, you will get the scoop on what that entails in the next chapter.

INFLUENCER OPPORTUNITIES

Being an influencer, which was mentioned in a prior chapter, can be a lucrative way to earn money from your blogging efforts. If you have a good following, you will most likely get businesses that want you to be an influencer for their product or service. You may also get invited to events because you are seen as an influencer.

I have been invited to influencer events. By attending these events, you will usually be paid for your time and your influence. The influencing comes into play because you will let people know you are attending the event. You may report from it or post from the event, and you will likely follow up with photos, video, a write-up, or a combination of those. The company that wants to pay you to be an influencer at an event will usually let you know what they want in exchange for it. They will tell you if they want you to post on Instagram, using a particular hashtag, or if you have free will to do as you please to share that you were at the event.

When you are approached by businesses to be an influencer at these events, be sure to home in on what is in it for you. They want you for a reason, because they believe you have a good following and you will influence your audience in their favor. But it has to be worth your time to attend, so be sure to check out what you will get for being a part of the event. If they are offering you a hundred dollars and you feel it's worth a lot more, don't hesitate to counteroffer and let them know what your fee is.

When you counteroffer, be sure to remind them of the audience that you have and why this rate is still a good deal for them. If you are offered three hundred dollars to attend a short event that is near home, you may feel that's a good exchange and take it without even considering a counteroffer. It's your time, your effort, and your blog and audience. Aim to get what you think it's worth for you to be an influencer. Don't sell yourself short. Having said that, some may offer you gift certificates or products in exchange for you being an influencer at their event. Again, it's up to you if you feel it's worth the exchange. If it sounds like a good arrangement to you, then go for it.

CAREER OPPORTUNITIES

You may set out to be a blogger and only a blogger, not having to work for someone else. But your blog has the potential to open career doors. Whether or not you are interested in them at this point, it will happen. If your blog becomes successful, which it will if you put in the effort and stick with it, businesses will see it. Blogging is a great way to enhance your résumé and professional profile.

If you are on LinkedIn or you are applying for a job, you will be able to tell people you are a blogger. The potential employer can look at your blog to see what kind of work you do. You never know what people will be reading your posts. Some can be hiring managers, business owners, or even headhunters, who are looking for someone with your skills and knowledge.

Blogging gives you skills that are an asset to a company. Not only do you learn blogging skills, but you will become a better writer, and you will gain great social media marketing skills. You could get hired as a blogger or social media expert at a business, or you could get job opportunities that are not related to blogging itself, but are related to the field you are blogging about. I'll say again that blogging helps you to become an expert of sorts on that topic or area.

When you have a blog, you will be establishing yourself as a professional, and anyone can take a look at it see for themselves what you are capable of. One quick search of your name, and you are likely to come up. This gives potential employers a way to check out your skills and personality. Your blogging skills may be the competitive edge that helps you get hired in a great position.

Your blogging may also help you get a foot in the door into a field that you may otherwise feel you lack the qualifications for. Let's say that you have great skills in a particular area, but you don't have a degree specifically in that area. Or you don't have a way to show you have official knowledge of the field. Your blog gives you an in-depth way to showcase your knowledge and abilities in that particular area. Plus, as a blogger, you will be seen by potential employers as a leader, which is always a good thing.

Not everyone may want their blog to lead to a great job. I get that, and having been self-employed since 2004, I can thoroughly understand it. Many people find that they like being self-employed and will stick with it long-term, but there are others who don't care for it. Being self-employed can be a roller-coaster ride at times, in all honesty. One week you can be swimming in cash, and for the next two weeks you barely have any coming in. You have to look at how much you make for the year and you have to be diligent in managing the cash flow throughout the year.

Additionally, being self-employed, if you are blogging as more than a side hustle, requires discipline. Unlike when you work for someone, you have to be your own source of motivation. You have to maintain a schedule of some sorts so that you make sure you meet deadlines and publish enough posts, and you have to make yourself sit in the chair and produce blog posts. Many people believe in writer's block, but I never have. I believe there is sitting your butt in the chair and getting the work done, and then there are excuses for not getting it done.

THE FUTURE OF YOUR BLOG

At this point, if you are just now starting your blog, you have no idea where it is going to take you. Nobody can tell that from the start. But knowing that there are so many possibilities that your blogging can lead to, it may inspire you, and it gives you things to watch for or move toward as your blog grows.

Your blogging can take you to creating numerous blogs, it can help you get a new job in the corporate world if you want one, or it can take you any number of other places. There are many possible directions your blog can take you, which is really exciting to think about. Blogging opens up a whole new world in the topic of your choice, and it's all up to you if you decide to enter it.

The good news is that you have control over the future of your blog. You will be able to make all the decisions regarding which direction you allow it to take you in. That's a good position to be in, because you will have some exciting and fun opportunities presented to you. Whether you take them all or not, it's nice to know what options you have and be able to make the final call.

BLOGGER SPOTLIGHT
Nicole Malik
Hook & Porter Media
www.hookporter.com

I am president of Hook & Porter Media, a digital publishing company with a current portfolio of eleven sites. The ones I personally write for still are my food blog (www.DeliciousEveryday.com) and my travel blog (www.Wandertooth.com).

When did you first start blogging and what got you interested in doing so?
I first got interested in blogging after reading *The 4-Hour Workweek* by Tim Ferriss many years ago. It exposed me to the world of online marketing and passive income.

I had a career in marketing that I truly loved and was very successful at, but knew that I had no interest in working for other people, for forty-plus hours per week, for the rest of my life. I started playing around with blogging as a hobby, and got serious about it around 2013.

What blogging format do you use, and are you happy with it?
I've always been on WordPress! There really isn't a comparable platform out there for blogging. You can build pretty much anything you want, with almost no development skills. It's quite remarkable.

How long did it take before you were making a good salary each year from your blog?

My financial journey with blogging has been a bit different from most bloggers. I've built a profitable portfolio very quickly by buying existing websites rather than building them from scratch.

I started blogging seriously in 2013. And while those initial websites are still going strong, the real value of those early days was in the education I got by running those sites. Once I felt confident in my skill set, I began thinking of how to scale the business most quickly. And for me, the answer was to acquire additional sites that already had some level of success. With fifteen-plus years of marketing experience at that time, I knew it would be easier and faster to grow existing businesses than build brand-new ones.

So when I was ready to take the leap from my corporate marketing career to full-time blogging, I acquired several additional sites to build out my portfolio. And then I doubled down on growing them. I was able to scale to a multi-six figure business within that first year.

What did you find to be your biggest challenge in blogging, and how did you overcome it?

Time. I went into buying and selling websites with the idea that they would be largely passive income. And that couldn't be further from the truth.

Blogging is a ton of work. Besides crafting great content, bloggers need to be social media managers, PR experts, website developers, video producers, and more. It's a lot of hats to wear.

The biggest step change in productivity came when I started hiring help. You don't need to be earning a ton of money to bring on help— you can start with a virtual assistant for just a few hours a week.

At this point I run a portfolio of eleven websites with the help of two full-time team members and many freelance writers.

What advice would you offer to new bloggers, or those who are still struggling to earn money from their blog?

Treat blogging like a business from the beginning, and you will see results much faster.

Many people start blogging by simply writing what they feel like writing, with no real plan for how people will find the content or how they will make money from it. Some of these people get lucky, and wind up making it work. Most of them don't.

Learn SEO (search engine optimization) from the start. You don't need to take a fancy course—there is more than enough free information out there to get started. Learn to write about the things your readers WANT to read, and learn how to optimize your content so people actually FIND it. If you do just this one thing, you will be miles ahead of most new bloggers.

What is one thing you have done that has helped you be able to earn more blogging?

Test, test, and test some more.

I see so many bloggers plugging along without a real understanding of what is driving their business. If you are going to learn just one tool, make it Google Analytics. Test relentlessly.

You'll be surprised at how much difference small tweaks can make to your income. Making your font size a bit larger may allow for more ad impressions on a page, generating more revenue. Moving an opt-in up a few paragraphs may grow your email list 20 percent faster. Adding a video may increase your dwell time by 10 percent, improving both revenue and search rankings.

This stuff adds up. I keep a running list of "experiments" that are in progress, and implement changes based on those results every week.

What is your top tip for bloggers who want to earn a salary from their blog?

Decide what you're going to invest: time or money. There's an old saying in the marketing world—"good, fast, cheap—pick two." And it pretty much applies to everything in business.

For many people starting out, investing money in the business isn't an option. And that's totally fine. But be prepared to invest your time. Don't expect your blog to be an overnight success, and don't be discouraged when things take longer than you would like.

Work smart. Don't fall into the trap of trying to do everything—you won't be able to. So pick the few things that generate the most impact and focus your time on those. For most new bloggers that means creating great content and learning the basics of SEO.

Focus on these things and you will see growth. And when the profits start to come, you can reinvest them to grow the business even faster.

11

Making Money by Blogging for Others

While many people have successful blogs of their own from which they make money, there are others who write blog posts for *other* people's blogs. Then there are people like me who happen to do both. If you enjoy writing blog posts, then writing for other people's blogs is another avenue that provides potential earnings. At this point you may not know if you want to blog for other people or not, but even so, it's a good idea to know the opportunity exists.

WHOM WOULD YOU BLOG FOR?

There are many companies that realize how beneficial it can be to have a blog. By having a blog, they can help to drive traffic to their website, where they are selling a product or service, and they can make a connection with more potential customers. Yet they may not have someone on their staff who wants to take on blogging. Some people may not have the time to add it to their list of duties, or they may not feel comfortable with blogging.

A blog can be an effective marketing tool. Plus, it's affordable to have one, and you get additional benefits beyond just marketing. A blog can help a company become established as an expert, expand upon services and products that they offer, provide additional helpful information beyond trying to sell the reader something, and can help with branding purposes. A blog, quite honestly, can become the voice of a company.

If a company realizes that they can benefit from having a blog and they don't have someone on staff that will become their blogger, they are faced with two options. The first is to hire someone to work at the company, and the second is to outsource the work to a blogger or writer. The first option can be quite costly—so much so that they may not feel they can justify hiring someone to do it in-house. A new employee means there will be a training program, a set salary, office space and supplies, taxes and insurance that needs to be paid on that employee, and so on.

On the other hand, outsourcing their blogging efforts will cost the company a fraction of what they would spend by hiring someone to work in their company. By outsourcing the work, they can pay only for the blog posts they need, skipping all the other expenses. Hiring a freelance blogger will help them to save money, as well as ensure they get a better return on investment for having a blog. They will also have flexibility when they work with a freelancer, ordering up blog posts when and if they are needed.

In addition to blogging for companies, you can also blog for individuals. There are successful bloggers who will hire bloggers to either contribute to their blog, or to ghostblog for them. There are opportunities in both areas for those who want to earn money by providing the service to other people.

OFFERING BLOGGING SERVICES

In order for you to start offering blogging services for other people, it's a good idea to have blogging experience. You should get your own blog up and running for a while before offering that type of service to others. Once you have run your own blog for a while, you will learn the best way to write blog posts, how to use your blogging platform, and what types of blog post topics do well with your audience. You will also learn how to come up with blog post ideas by that point. These are all skills that you will put to use blogging for others.

For years, I've provided blogging services for other people and businesses. I have written blog posts for some clients that I have had for well over five years. Not only do I write blog posts ongoing for businesses, but I also do it for individuals. Most of the writing that I do for other blogs is considered ghostwriting, or ghostblogging. This means that my name doesn't go on it as the author. In fact, it means I'm a ghost other than doing the work and being paid for it.

Once you write blog posts for a company when you are ghostwriting for them, you should not share that information with other people. My friends and family don't even know who it is that I write blog posts for. I take ghostwriting seriously and would not divulge that information to people. It's unethical to agree to be a ghostwriter and then share that information with people, telling them who you are writing for. If you are a ghostwriter, be a ghostwriter. Your relationship starts and ends with the client, and everything in between and outside of that is kept confidential.

Having said that, you will want to be able to build your blogger portfolio so you can show others what you are capable of. Not only is this another good reason to have a blog of your own, but you should try to get a few clients where it isn't considered ghostwriting. That way you can add those to your portfolio to provide people with samples of your blogging work.

Some people, such as myself, have no problem with the idea of ghostwriting for others. But there are others who take exception to it. Some people don't care for it, because they want their name on things, they want to be able to add it to their portfolio and take credit for it, and some just feel it's not right for a variety of other reasons. Well, to be honest with you, ghostwriting is commonplace. There are many books in the bookstore that are written by ghostwriters and you don't even realize it. The same goes for blogs, magazine articles, and so on.

Everyone has skills in some area, but not everyone feels comfortable with their writing skills. Those people may want to hire a writer. Still others may have writing skills, but lack the time in their professional lives to add in writing articles or other materials. For whatever reason, they prefer to outsource their writing projects. I'm perfectly comfortable doing ghostwriting projects for others. I understand why people and businesses hire writers, I don't feel slighted by not getting my name on it or being recognized as the writer, and I enjoy the income I get from all the ghostwriting.

At this point, I write for numerous blogs ongoing, and I've ghostwritten eight books for professionals. My kids, even as teenagers, say that they don't understand why I don't mind someone else's name going on a book as the author of the book that I wrote. That's when I remind them once again that they never mind the money I made from it paying for things like their travel soccer bills. That usually ends the discussion until it comes up again at a later time.

HOW TO GET BLOGGING JOBS

If you want to offer blogging services for others, you have to be able to connect with those who are looking for the service. You can do that through a variety of ways. For starters, you should have the information posted somewhere online, such as in an online portfolio. Whether you have a freelance blogging website where you offer information about your services and experiences, or you add a page to your blog that shares that information, it's important to get it out there.

Give people a clear and easy way to contact you about your services. Having a way to contact you seems like a no-brainer, but you would be surprised how many people overlook it. When I was looking for bloggers to be included in the "blogger spotlight" areas in this book, I visited many blogs. Numerous ones had no way that I could see for me to contact the blogger to inquire if they would be interested in participating. There was no contact form, no email address, nothing. So make it a priority to have a way for people to contact you once you have made it known that you offer blogging services.

You can also find blogging clients by looking at job boards. Such sites as Guru.com and UpWork.com have job boards where those who need bloggers post what they need. You can then come along, read their job post, and submit a quote as to how much you will charge and what your time frame for doing the work would be.

Let me be the first to tell you that there are a lot of crappy jobs on these boards. You will come across jobs where they are offering people one to three dollars per blog post for your writing services. You have to skip over all those crappy jobs and look for the ones that are decent or good. There are some good ones on there, but you have to really sift through to find them. Once you do find them, if you get the project, you could keep that same client for years to come.

You can also approach businesses yourself, offering your blogging services. You can do this by email, in person, telephone, networking, or through any other means you see possible. Prepare something you can provide to them that lets the company know what you offer, why they may want to outsource their blogging (or why they should start a blog that you will do the blogging for), where they can get more information and see samples of your work, and how they can contact you.

A good way to find local companies to blog for is to join your local chamber of commerce. They usually hold a monthly mixer type of event, where you can network with other small-business owners in your area. This is a great time to hand out business cards and let them know you are a freelance blogger and what your services entail.

There are other ways you can find blogging jobs, too, including advertising your services. You can also use your blogging skills to write blog posts that bring you potential clients. Get creative and try different methods to see what works for you. Always track where your clients come from, so that you will know what method of marketing your services is working. That way you put more of your efforts into that method, rather than other methods that are not paying off.

WRITING FOR OTHERS

When you are writing posts for someone else, whether it's a company or an individual, you need to tailor your writing so that it sounds like it's coming from them, rather than you. This means you need to capture their voice and style. Everyone has their own style, voice, and preferences. They will want their blog posts to sound like they are something that came from their company, as opposed to coming from outside of it from a freelancer.

Keeping this in mind, you will want to do a little homework before writing the posts for your clients. Look over their website to learn about their products or services. You need to know what it is that they sell or do, what their company stands for, and about their history. It's also important to know who their target market is. Knowing this information will help you write blog posts that will help them meet their objectives of having a blog.

If you are unable to tell these things from your own research, dig deeper. Send them a short list of questions that they can answer on the topic. This gives them a chance to tell you what is important to them and what kind of person is their ideal customer. Doing things like this will help you capture their voice.

It also helps to know what their preferences are when it comes to their blog posts. Do they want you to come up with ideas for each post? If so, do you need to have them approved first? Or will they supply you with blog post ideas? Other things you will want to know include what word count they prefer, how many blog posts they want per week or month, and what you will be paid for each post.

Some of these questions they may not have an answer for. They simply may not be that familiar with it all to know what to tell you. In those cases, you should be prepared to offer suggestions to them. You may find that some clients want to order up twenty blog posts or more at a time, which they will take and then schedule out on their blog. Others may want you to submit one or two blog posts per week, or every other week. It's important to find out their schedule preferences if this will be an ongoing project.

When it comes to getting paid, you can have them either pay you through PayPal or send a check. Those are the two most popular options, although you could also find others to consider. I've even been offered Bitcoin to write posts. Whether or not you take something like that and how you go about getting paid is to be worked out between you and the client, but you should both feel comfortable with the arrangement.

When working with a new client, most writers will want to be paid something up front. It's common for you to ask for half up front before you begin the project, and then the balance upon submitting it. There are other clients who are happy to pay for the whole project up front, and still others who you may just bill once you submit the work. I often bill new clients at least half up front, and then once I have written for them for a while, I will start billing them after I submit the work. Doing this helps to protect you, should they try to skip out on paying anything.

Now, let's get to the burning question of how much to charge for your blog post writing services. This is something that you will have to determine based off of what you are comfortable making per hour or post. I always quote my writing jobs per project, giving them a flat fee, rather than by hour. I don't care for the hourly method of giving someone a quote. I know about how long it takes me to write something, and then I determine a rate per blog post from there.

You will want to consider other factors when coming up with your blog post rate, too. Additional things to consider include whether or not you will be doing the work to log into their blogging platform and set up each post, and if you will have to find an image to go with each one. Each of these extra steps will take you more time, so you want to consider that when quoting the project. I have clients that I have done the blog posting for within their platform, but I much prefer to write the posts, send them to the client, and then be hands-off from there.

Another thing you may want to consider is whether or not you will provide a volume discount. You may have clients who approach you who want to place an order for fifty to a hundred blog posts at one time. Since they are giving you a large order, they will at times ask if you will provide them with a volume discount. Again, this is something that is your call, because you need to be comfortable with your earnings per post. Personally speaking, I will usually try to give them a small volume discount so that I am working with them on the price and we both feel good about the amount in the end.

There is no set amount that you can earn from writing each blog post. The rates are all over the board, based upon blogger experience, the time you will invest, what company you are writing for, and what all will be involved. Some bloggers may be comfortable earning thirty dollars per blog post, while others may ask for a hundred or more per post. The bottom line is that the rate you settle upon has to be one you are comfortable with. If it is, then what your fee is makes no difference if others feel it's too low or too high. It's your time, your salary, and your call.

SOURCES AND RIGHTS

When you are blogging for others, you want to use the same kind of rules you would use when blogging for yourself. Use professional sources if you are citing information, and follow the rules and guidelines that were mentioned earlier in the book in regard to plagiarism, libel, and keeping your posts legal.

The money you earn from blogging for other people you will have to include in your yearly income taxes, just the same as the money you earn from your own blog. Some people who hire you to write for them may provide you with a tax form when the time comes, but most tend not to. It all depends on how much you earn from that particular client, and how you got paid. If you were paid through PayPal, for example, you can obtain a yearly tax statement showing earnings through their system. The same goes for jobs you do through the job board sites that have been mentioned in this chapter.

While you are writing the blog posts for others, you are not going to end up owning the rights to those. Since you are being hired to do it for other people or businesses, the rights to the article or post are going to go with the article. In other words, the person who paid for you to write for their blog will be the copyright owner, unless you have worked out some other arrangement. It's standard, however, for the rights to stay with the person or company that owns the blog and has paid for the work.

If you want a post of yours to go on someone else's blog and you get your name on there and possibly a link to your blog, that's guest blogging. That topic was discussed in chapter 4 as a possible way to promote your blog. There are some sites that will pay for guest posts and give you the byline, but you will have to actively seek those opportunities out and come up with topics that will fit their blog and try to sell your posts piecemeal. Keep in mind that many people who purchase guest posts want unique content that hasn't been posted anywhere else, and that won't be posted elsewhere.

Blogging for others is one more way to earn money as a blogger. Whether you seek out the opportunities or they tend to come to you, they can add up to a great salary and open more doors.

BLOGGER SPOTLIGHT
Cristy Stewart-Harfmann
Happy Family Blog
www.happyfamilyblog.com

When did you first start blogging and what got you interested in doing so?
I started blogging five years ago. When my daughter was born I was working for an agency working a hundred hours a week. I found I was missing my daughter growing up. I wanted to have a creative outlet that allowed me to use my marketing skills and have a flexible schedule. Blogging has done exactly that for me.

What blogging format do you use, and are you happy with it?
I use WordPress and highly recommend them.

How long did it take before you were making a good salary each year from your blog?
It took a year before I made any money and two years before I was making a full-time salary. Five years ago there was less information about how to make money so I was flying blind and learned by trial and error.

What did you find to be your biggest challenge in blogging, and how did you overcome it?
Blogging means you work for yourself so you don't have a boss keeping you on track. The most unexpected part of my blogging journey has been the friendships I have made. These friends have helped get be inspired during times where I need the extra push.

What advice would you offer to new bloggers, or those who are still struggling to earn money from their blog?
There are so many ways to make money blogging; be open to them all. Having multiple streams of income is essential to have long-term success.

What is one thing you have done that has helped you be able to earn more blogging?

I focused on growing a community on Instagram. It helped me focus on improving my photography. By focusing a majority of my effort in one channel I was able to really grow the platform. With blogging, it is easy to get pulled into lots of different directions between SEO, Pinterest, Facebook, Twitter, Instagram, TikTok, etc. It is important to learn them all, but you may want to focus on one channel to master first.

What is your top tip for bloggers who want to earn a salary from their blog?

Be authentic and grow a community. It is easy to see what other people are doing and want to try to do that too, but if it is not authentic to you, it is not worth it.

12

Connecting with Other Bloggers

If you make your living as a blogger, you will find that you may feel a bit secluded at times. If you are an introvert like me, you probably won't mind that too much. But even as an introvert, I also like to meet up with people once in a while. Sure, I may need to quickly get back to the comfort of my home office and decompress, but once in a while it's nice to catch up with others and learn what is new in the world of blogging.

It's a good idea to try to connect with other bloggers. By doing so, you will be able to learn new things, share what you know, network, and chat with people who get what you are doing. And you get what they are doing. As a blogger, it's nice to be able to get together with others and talk about blogging. When you do this, you can share what everyone is working on, if there is anything new they have discovered, or if they have found new or better ways of earning money from their blogging.

I have been blogging for over a decade and I enjoy meeting up once in a while with other bloggers to chat. I never feel that because I have been doing it so long there is nothing I need from that group or conversation. I do find things I can take from those conversations and I'm always open to learning more about blogging. As I've shared in this book, there are some blogging issues that are controversial. We don't all agree on how you should do particular things, and that's okay. It's nice to even be able to discuss those things that we bloggers tend to have varied views on. Even if I don't decide to take their path or incorporate what they are doing, I enjoy hearing about all the possibilities.

There are numerous ways you can connect with other bloggers. You certainly don't have to do them all. But if you pick one or two to try out, you may find that you enjoy the interaction with other bloggers. Where you live can also play a role in what types of blogging networking are at your disposal. If you live in a rural area, for example, it may be difficult for you to find a monthly blogging group to attend. But you will still find other options to consider.

Connecting with other bloggers will help keep you inspired and keep you learning and growing. As long as everyone is an established blogger, everyone will end up getting something out of the connection. If, on the other hand, your group is open to people who are in the process of starting their blog, you may feel like you are just providing a lot of guidance at each meeting. This can become taxing if you feel like you show up every month and just tell someone how to start and grow their blog, and how to make money from blogging.

I understand not wanting to turn new bloggers away, but you may want to have one special hour per meeting or a special new blogger night every once in a while. That way new bloggers can attend at those times. This will help break them in, without the focus of every meetup being the basics of how to get started.

You have to get something out of the group or you won't want to continue going for long. Your blogging network group should be a win-win for everyone who attends. It should help to support and inspire one another.

If you are a new blogger and want to learn from other local bloggers, find one that you may be able to shadow. Contact the person to see how they feel about you shadowing them a bit, or them being a mentor to you, so that they can help show you the ropes.

BLOGGER MEETUPS

Depending on where you live, you may be able to find blogger meetup groups. These are organized groups of local bloggers who meet up, usually once a month. The group will discuss a variety of topics that relate to blogging. You may be able to find these on Meetup.com, in Facebook groups, or elsewhere.

Since there was no blogging meetup in my area, I had started one on Facebook with a fellow blogger. There were about twenty people who joined. However, hardly anyone attended. We had a couple of people who dropped in to try to learn about blogging, but most people never attended any meetings. After a while we axed the group, because we felt that in our area, which is smaller, there was a lack of interest in having a blogger meetup group.

Larger cities will likely do well by having this type of group. I have seen some online in other cities that are an hour or two away from where I am, and they have many members and they likely get a good turnout. Even if you live in a smaller area, if this type of group interests you, then you should at least try starting one if one doesn't already exist. If there is no interest or you can't find other local bloggers, then you can always do away with it and move on to something else.

The bloggers you make connections with do not need to be in the same genre as you are. If you want to find bloggers who blog about the same types of things, that's fine, but it's also a good idea to connect with those who blog about different topics. You can learn and share with other bloggers, despite what they blog about, so don't feel you should limit yourself to only connecting with bloggers who cover the same niche.

ATTENDING CONFERENCES

There are blogging conferences and workshops that take place around the country. It is especially good to attend these if you are new to blogging. You can learn a great deal about blogging and are able to meet up and chat with other bloggers. You can check their itinerary to see if there are events or segments at the conferences that appeal to you.

If you are a seasoned blogger, you may want to consider being a presenter at these events. Conferences always need successful bloggers to give presentations to those who are attending. Some pay for your participation, or will pick up travel expenses, while others may only provide free entry into the rest of the conference.

There is a blogger conference that takes place every year about an hour from where I live, called Florida BlogCon. I have attended twice, but it's almost always scheduled on my daughter's birthday weekend, and I won't attend it instead of being with her on her birthday. I still take a look each year though, so I can see what date it has been scheduled for, and if there are any workshops at it that I want to check out.

If I had the funds, I'd love to travel to some other blogging conferences that are farther away. I realize that I could apply to be a speaker or presenter at these events. I have read the call for speakers before, but I haven't yet felt compelled to apply.

ONLINE GROUPS

There are numerous online blogging groups that you can join. I've seen quite a few on Facebook, and I have joined a few of them to see what they are about. I went into them thinking that they would be groups where bloggers have discussions about blogging. However, the groups I've joined haven't turned out like that at all.

The blogging groups I've joined on Facebook have been about promoting your blog. By that, I mean that you are posting links to your blog posts in the group. So all the bloggers are posting links to their new posts, which makes me wonder if any of the other bloggers are actually clicking on the links to check the post out. And would they even be the target market—would the post be of interest to this random group of people?

I'm still on the hunt for a good online blogging group where bloggers can chat. Not one where we are all promoting our blog post links to one another, or where the person who has the group is trying to sell you on their blogging boot camp course. I'm still hopeful of finding a group like this. I could start one, but I am trying not to become the admin for yet one more thing that would tie me to social media. As a member, I can check it out when I want; as an admin, you have more responsibility, including moderating posts and members.

If you are not finding the types of blogging meetups, workshops, and groups that you would like to belong to, consider starting them yourself. There may be other people in your area who would be interested in joining them, but someone needs to be the first one to get them started.

KEEP LEARNING

Technology moves fast, as you likely know. Just when you think you have figured out how to do something, a part of it will be changed. The technology will be updated or removed all together. There's no telling what is going to happen with the future of blogging. Things will change in the world of blogging; that's the one thing we can rely upon.

Over the time I have been blogging, there have been numerous changes that have taken place with blogging. I've had to learn through each one and find my way around it. When there are things that come up that you need to address, you work your way through it and get them taken care of. Whether it's getting a message from your advertising network that changes are on the way, or Google requires that your blog become responsive, you just have to work your way through them.

My favorite psychology professor in college used to say that life is a problem-solving process. Every day we are confronted with problems. Those problems change throughout time. At one time, you didn't know how to walk, talk, tie your shoes, type, and so on. We continue to overcome new problems and challenges all of the time. If we don't, we become stagnant and will be left behind.

It's important to be flexible as a blogger. Be ready to make changes. Instead of fighting them, figure them out. You will be able to and you will be happy that you figured out a way to overcome any challenges. And believe me, every blogger has had to contend with challenges. Whether it has been learning the technical side of blogging, getting comfortable with writing blog posts, or finding a way to best market their site, every successful blogger has faced such challenges head-on.

INVEST IN YOURSELF

If you want to become a successful blogger, you have to invest in yourself. This goes for anything you want to do in life. If you have to spend money on a book, class, hosting, or other things, it's all an investment in yourself. You will be gaining the skills you need to become a successful blogger, or to become a *more* successful blogger.

If you want to be a successful blogger who is earning money from your efforts, you can be. It all starts with a positive mind. It was Henry Ford who said, "Whether you think you can or you can't—you're right." Having a positive outlook and believing in yourself and what you are doing is essential. It will help you overcome challenges and be willing to learn new things, and will keep you going when you start to question yourself.

At first, blogging may seem like it's difficult to do. That's because you have a learning curve, but if you stick with it, you will learn the ins and outs of it, and it will become like second nature. If you have been blogging for a while now and at times question what and why you are blogging, hopefully this book has given you some things to think about to overcome that hump.

Whether you are getting ready to start a blog, you have been blogging for a while and haven't been earning money, or you are a blogger who does earn a salary from your efforts, my hope is that you take away some nuggets of information from this book that you can put to use. Every blogger that has been doing it for a while will have a different story to tell about how they do it and what has worked for them. There is no right and wrong way to do it; there are just different ways. Learn as much as you can from as many bloggers as you can, so that you can see what will work for you and your blog.

I wish you success in your blogging adventure and hope that you, too, will be making a comfortable salary from your blogging efforts before you know it. Blog on!

About the Author

Jacqueline Bodnar has been a professional writer and blogger since 2004. She has ghostwritten eight books, published four in her name, and published over 3,000 articles in newspapers and magazines. She blogs extensively, having numerous popular blogs of her own, as well as ghostblogging for other companies and individuals. Jacqueline holds a bachelor of arts degree in social science studies and a master of professional writing degree. When she's not writing and blogging, she enjoys hiking, camping, snorkeling, and reading. She lives with her husband and two children in the Daytona Beach, Florida, area.

Index

C

Canva, 30, 39, 79, 99
career, opportunities, 109–110
click-through, rate, 40
coaching, services, 52, 53, 108
cookies, 77
comments, 88–90
communication
    email, 90–91
Communications Decency Act, 75
conferences, 51, 105–106, 127
consistency, 22, 69, 85–86
content
    creating, 54
    evergreen, 30, 54, 69
    goals, 83–85
    quality, 16, 43, 45, 54
contributing bloggers, 101
copyright, 78–80
copywriting, 97
cost per thousand (CPM), 50
corporations, blogging for, 32
courses, selling, 52
crawlers, 60
custom logo, 99–100

D

design, 99–100
disclosures, 76–77
domain, registration, 5, 9

E

email communication, 90–91
enhancing your blog
    add a profile page, 95–96
    copywriting skills, 97
    custom logo, 99–100
    media kit, 100

photography skills, 96–97
    plug-ins, 6, 8, 59, 98–99
    using video, 97–98
entry page, 65
events
    hosting, 54
evergreen topics, 30
exit page, 65

F

Facebook, 19, 22, 36, 37, 38, 39, 41, 42,
    75, 87, 89, 123, 126, 127, 128
fair use, 79
Federal Trade Commission (FTC),
    76, 77
first blog, 2, 13, 25, 26
focus, of blog, 3–4
following, building a, 83–94

G

getting paid, 72–73
Google
    Ads, 42, 50
    Adsense, 65, 67, 77, 99
    Analytics, 57, 61–62, 113
    Analytics Academy, 62
    News, 18
    PageSpeed Insights, 63
    Submit URL, 60
    Tools, 62–63
    Trends, 18
Groups, 91–92
guest posts, 11, 40–41, 92, 121

H

headlines, 28
hosting, services, 6, 7, 9

Books from Allworth Press

Brand Thinking and Other Noble Pursuits
by Debbie Millman with foreword by Rob Walker (6 × 9, 336 pages, paperback, $19.95)

Branding for Bloggers
by Zach Heller with the New York Institute of Career Development (5½ × 8¼, 112 pages, paperback, $16.95)

Feng Shui and Money (Second Edition)
by Eric Shaffert (6 × 9, 256 pages, paperback, $19.99)

From Idea to Exit (Revised Edition)
by Jeffrey Weber (6 × 9, 272 pages, paperback, $19.95)

Fund Your Dreams Like a Creative Genius™
by Brainard Carey (6⅛ × 6⅛, 160 pages, paperback, $12.99)

The Global PR Revolution
by Maxim Behar (6 × 9, 312 pages, hardcover, $29.99)

The Law (in Plain English)® for Small Business (Fifth Edition)
by Leonard D. DuBoff and Amanda Bryan (6 × 9, 312 pages, paperback, $24.99)

Legal Guide to Social Media
by Kimberly A. Houser (6 × 9, 208 pages, paperback, $19.95)

Millennial Rules
by T. Scott Gross (6 × 9, 176 pages, paperback, $16.95)

The Money Mentor
by Tad Crawford (6 × 9, 272 pages, paperback, $24.95)

The Online Writer's Companion
by P. J. Aitken (6 × 9, 344 pages, paperback, $19.99)

Profit from Your Podcast
by Dave Jackson (6 × 9, 192 pages, paperback, $16.99)

The Profitable Artist (Second Edition)
by The New York Foundation for the Arts (6 × 9, 288 pages, paperback, $24.99)

The Secret Life of Money
by Tad Crawford (5½ × 8½, 304 pages, paperback, $19.95)

Sell Online Like a Creative Genius™
by Brainard Carey (6⅛ × 6⅛, 160 pages, paperback, $12.99)

Starting Your Career as a Freelance Writer (Third Edition)
by Moira Allen (6 × 9, 368 pages, paperback, $19.99)

Succeed with Social Media Like a Creative Genius™
by Brainard Carey (6⅛ × 6⅛, 144 pages, paperback, $12.99)

Website Branding for Small Businesses
by Nathalie Nahai (6 × 9, 288 pages, paperback, $19.95)

To see our complete catalog or to order online, please visit www.allworth.com.